LEADER

THE 5 W'S

WHO * WHAT * WHERE * WHEN * WHY

of Our Catholic Faith
LEARNING TO LOVE

LEADER

THE 5 W'S

WHO * WHAT * WHERE * WHEN * WHY

# of Our Catholic Faith
LEARNING TO LOVE

Experts Write About Christian Love

Liguori

LIGUORI, MISSOURI

Imprimi Potest: Harry Grile, CSsR
Provincial, Denver Province, The Redemptorists

Imprimatur:
Printed with Ecclesiastical Permission and Approved for Private or Instructional Use

Nihil Obstat: Reverend Erik T. Pohlmeier
               Censor Librorum
Imprimatur: + Anthony B. Taylor
               Bishop of Little Rock [Arkansas]
               June 17, 2013

Published by Liguori Publications
Liguori, Missouri 63057
To order, call 800-325-9521 or visit www.liguori.org.

Library of Congress Cataloging-in-Publication Data

The 5 W's of our Catholic faith : learning to love (leader).—First Edition.
    pages cm
 ISBN 978-0-7648-2398-5
1. Love—Religious aspects—Catholic Church—Study and teaching. 2. Catholic Church—Doctrines—Study and teaching. I. Liguori Publications. II. Title: Five W's of our Catholic faith.
 BV4639.A15 2013b
 268'.82—dc23
                    2013015679

p ISBN: 978-0-7648-2398-5
e ISBN: 978-0-7648-6842-9

Liguori Publications, a nonprofit corporation, is an apostolate of the Redemptorists. To learn more about the Redemptorists, visit Redemptorists.com.

Printed in the United States of America
17 16 15 14 13 / 5 4 3 2 1
First edition

Contents

Introduction

This final book in a series invites you to examine Catholic belief and practice through the lens of love.

*T*he *5 W's of Our Catholic Faith: Learning to Love* completes Liguori Publications' *5 W's* adult faith formation series. The three books in this series build on each other to provide a program of faith formation that engages the participants progressively in an examination of the basic tenets of the teaching of Jesus and his Church through the lens of the three theological virtues: faith, hope, and love. These virtues, which are also divine gifts, allow us to share directly in God's very nature—thereby enabling us to live lives in greater conformity with God's will and thus attain the eternal life he promises to give us (see the *Catechism of the Catholic Church* 1812–1813).

The series' first book, *The 5 W's of Our Catholic Faith and How We Live It*, focuses on the core content of the Catholic faith. It provides the participants with basic information and the opportunity to reflect on Church teaching, thus helping them find answers to many of their initial questions about the *5 W's*, the who, what, where, when, and why of our faith—and how to live it.

The second book, *The 5 W's of Our Catholic Faith: Living in Hope*, builds on the first. It revisits the teaching of the Church and how we live it, but from a different perspective: through the lens of hope, thus helping participants see how the grace of God has been at work in these areas in their own lives and in the Church throughout history. This second part of the series leads participants to a deeper and more personal embrace of their faith, better enabling them to connect what they believe with what they do, especially in the Eucharist, and furthering their ongoing intellectual and moral conversion.

This third book, *The 5 W's of Our Catholic Faith: Learning to Love*, invites participants to examine Catholic belief and practice through the lens of love, which Saint Paul identifies as the greatest of the theological virtues: "So faith, hope, love remain, these three; but the greatest of these is love" (1 Corinthians 13:13).

Since sacrificial love is God's very nature, it is also at the heart of his plan for our salvation. Faith is the foundation of our hope, and if genuine these lead to love that is real and "enfleshed"—just as God's love became enfleshed in the person of Jesus Christ. Love is the reason for Jesus' Incarnation and his embrace of the cross for our redemption—no mere abstraction, or else we would not be saved. Love is also the reason he founded the Church and continues to send us forth to bring the Good News of Jesus Christ to people who still live in darkness and the shadow of death today—that same love "enfleshed" in us. Christian love is not just about warm feelings; it is a commitment that requires death to self.

Taken together, these three volumes have the goal of enabling the participants to draw on their faith and God's grace to do just that: to live lives of sacrificial love. For many people this begins with them taking a more active role in the work of the Lord in their parish and in the larger community. To do this effectively, they must be familiar not only with the teaching of Jesus and his Church, but also with the human and social environment into which Jesus sends them to undertake the badly needed New Evangelization.

God has blessed the Church with many resources to help us learn and reflect upon his will for our lives, including sacred Scripture, the Liturgy of the Church, the witness of countless saints in every age, the insights of theologians and the authoritative teaching of the Church's magisterium. In recent times the teaching of the Second Vatican Council—and the *Catechism of the Catholic Church*, which summarizes Church teaching in the light of the council—continue to serve as especially helpful guides for us as we bring the teaching of Jesus and his Church to bear on the issues we face today.

Among the key teachings of Vatican II that have proven especially helpful for people on their own faith journey and for the larger mission of the Church are: (1) its desire to foster greater love for and knowledge of sacred Scripture, (2) its vision of a united and interdependent world, (3) its emphasis on the universal call to holiness that should characterize the spiritual quest of every human being, and (4) the proclamation of God's kingdom by all believers who work to foster peace and justice, forgiveness and healing in today's world and in individual lives. And, as the participants in this third and final part of this *5 W's* series will learn, this can only be achieved through sacrificial love: lives built on faith and hope rooted in the very love of God himself.

+Bishop Anthony B. Taylor

Diocese of Little Rock

How to Use This Program

Like its predecessors, this book's ten sessions can be broken down in a variety of ways.

- Present a session a month for ten months.

- The sessions can be set up during Advent and Lent, once a week for the four weeks of Advent and six weeks of Lent.

- Schedule a session every two weeks over a five-month span to allow for personal reading of the material before the session.

- Several sessions can be used for a weekend retreat: for example, three, four, or five sessions used for a full-day gathering; two to three sessions for a 9 a.m. to 1 p.m. meeting or for a full weekend retreat, two sessions on Friday evening, and four each on Saturday and Sunday. (Here you might consider eliminating the opening prayers, readings, and concluding prayers.)

- No matter how the sessions are covered, a condition for quality discussion requires people to read the material and answer the five questions before the session.

- With all of these settings, keep in mind the importance of allowing time for socializing. While some participants may come simply for the education, most will appreciate the opportunity to speak with others who are gathered there. Especially with longer meetings and certainly with a retreat, think about providing refreshments, maybe even a meal, if appropriate.

Notes to leaders

- Establish a calendar for how long *The 5 W's of Our Catholic Faith: Learning to Love* sessions will run and present the schedule when the program is announced.

- Allow for at least seventy-five minutes per session.

- Review all the material to be covered beforehand.

- Have the meeting space prepared ahead of time and ready for the opening prayer.

- Have name tags ready for the first couple of sessions.

- Establish written ground rules (for example, do not let one person dominate the discussion; invite everyone to share; this is not a time to debate or argue, etc.).

- Keep discussion on any one topic limited. Allot the same amount of time for any single discussion; this will ensure that the majority of the material is covered.

- The sessions are laid out in an easy-to-use format and are designed to run for an hour and a half to two hours.

Once the session has begun

- After the hospitality, welcome, and opening (including the opening prayer), ask participants to share their answers to the five questions for that session. From there, move into each section using the **LOVE in Action** questions in addition to questions that may have arisen after the first reading.

- The timing of each section is flexible, depending on your needs, and can stretch from ten to thirty minutes per section. If you choose to have more time for each section, you may want to use the catechism quotes and other supporting material to add to the reflection and discussion.

- When the content has been covered, move on to the Closing Rite. Give participants a chance to pray for individual needs, and be mindful of any current events or situations that can be incorporated into the concluding prayer. Bless those gathered, sending them forth with the light of Christ in their hearts and spiritual food for the journey.

A note about suggested movies

Catholics have a long history of using virtues to help orient their lives. However, non-Christians have lived exemplary lives as well as they discern how to live lives of justice and peace. We are encouraged to find where God's kingdom is breaking forth in the world and celebrate its coming. Movies are a way to take the message of the Gospel to wider audiences. To make for a deeper study of the practice of love, especially sacrificial love, we have included at least one movie suggestion at the end of each chapter, in the "suggested resources" portions of the participant guide. Some of the films are inspired by religious events; others show men, women, and children witnessing the virtue of love in their daily lives.

Notes to participants

- Participants should come to class having answered the five questions (who, what, where, when, and why) as best as they could before reading.

- Come having read the material before class, underlining, highlighting or circling terms or narrative you might have a question about.

- Come with an open mind and heart, ready to follow the instructions of the leader.

- Don't dominate or argue. Listen respectfully and know when the answer to a question is not to be found in this forum.

The Mystery of the Church: Our Shared Journey Forward

By Johan van Parys, PhD

Preparation

Have ready a Bible, a candle, matches, and a cross or Christian icon. Set these up on a small table in front of the room where the group will meet, or in the center if you are using a circle format.

Optional

Prepare some simple refreshments for the group to share either before or after the session.

Have music playing quietly in the background on a CD or iPod as participants arrive and settle in.

Opening *TEN MINUTES*

When everyone is seated, light the candle. Begin with the suggested opening song or use one of your choosing. Or you can go directly to the opening prayer found in the session and have everyone read it aloud together.

Scripture Reading

Colossians 1:15–23

Ask a member of the group to read, or you can read it aloud to the group. Once the passage is read, direct group members to silently reflect for a minute or two on what they have just heard. This also serves as a centering and quieting exercise for participants.

Supporting catechism quotes for Session One:

"The Church is one because of her source: 'the highest exemplar and source of this mystery is the unity, in the Trinity of Persons, of one God, the Father and the Son in the Holy Spirit'" (CCC 813); UR 2 #5.

"From the first community of Jerusalem until the parousia, it is the same Paschal mystery that the Churches of God, faithful to the apostolic faith, celebrate in every place. The mystery celebrated in the liturgy is one, but the forms of its celebration are diverse" (CCC 1200).

"The liturgical traditions or rites presently in use in the Church are the Latin (principally the Roman rite, but also the rites of certain local churches, such as the Ambrosian rite, or those of certain religious orders) and the Byzantine, Alexandrian or Coptic, Syriac, Armenian, Maronite and Chaldean rites" (CCC 1203).

The Mystery of the Church

ALLOW FIFTEEN MINUTES FOR EACH SECTION.

Take a few minutes for the group to read through the section, then move to the **LOVE in Action** questions. Allow each person a minute or two to contribute, and give each group member the opportunity to speak.

Additional questions for reflection and discussion

- *As Catholics, we believe that our participation in the mystery of salvation is the greatest gift we will ever receive. How can we grow the awareness of our participation in the mystery of salvation? How does it change our outlook on the world?*

- *In our increasingly more complex, secularized, and individualistic world, speaking about the mystery of salvation is neither easy nor popular. How can we find ways to testify to our faith in a world that is increasingly indifferent at best and antagonistic at worst?*

- *If we allow ourselves to look beyond our own small world, we cannot help but notice that the Church is characterized more so by diversity than uniformity. Is this a gift to the Church? If so, how can we better embrace the rich diversity within our Church as an expression of the divine mystery?*

Closing Rite

FIVE MINUTES

Invite participants to take a few moments of silence, then ask the participants for spontaneous prayer. When finished, you can offer this brief blessing to the group:

The LORD bless you and keep you!

The LORD let his face shine upon you, and be gracious to you!

The LORD look upon you kindly and give you peace! (Numbers 6: 24–26)

Concluding Prayer: Ever-living God, Creator of all that is, in your goodness you have given us the gift of your Son as our paschal mystery. Through his death and resurrection, light has destroyed darkness and life has triumphed over death. Through our baptism you have adopted us as your sons and daughters and made us participants in his death and resurrection. Inspire us to more fully acknowledge your tremendous gift, let us live our lives more worthy of this gift, and send us out into the world to testify more vigorously to this gift. We ask this through our Lord Jesus Christ, your Son, our Passover and our hope, who lives with you in the unity of the Holy Spirit, one God forever and ever. Amen.

SESSION 1

The Mystery of the Church: Our Shared Journey Forward

By Johan van Parys, PhD

WHO created and sustains the Church?

WHAT mysteries of God do we encounter through faith in Jesus?

WHERE and how do we enter into divine life?

WHEN will we fully know and understand divine mysteries?

WHY do we need the sacraments?

Opening Song: "Bring Forth the Kingdom," by Marty Haugen, or a hymn of your choice

Opening Prayer: Ever-loving God, we thank you for the marvels of creation and for the mystery of salvation. Touch our hearts so we may embrace your unending love for us and enlighten our minds so we may better testify to your presence among us. We ask this through Christ, our Lord. Amen.

Reading: Colossians 1:15–23 (the preeminence of Christ)

Spend a moment in quiet reflection.

What Is Mystery?

The word "mystery" has enjoyed different meanings over the course of history. Even today, different people use the "mystery" in different ways. Etymologically speaking, "mystery" comes from the Greek *mysterion,* meaning "secret rite or doctrine." *Mysterion,* in turn, is derived from the Greek word *myein,* meaning "to close or to shut." The word "mystery" thus carries the notion of "sealed lips" and "closed eyes," implying that those who have been initiated into the mystery keep quiet about it, while those who have not been initiated are blind to it.

In today's popular culture, the word "mystery" refers to something unknown that needs to be solved. A perfect example of this usage is a murder mystery. In this kind of book or movie, the lead detective is expected to solve the mystery. What makes reading or watching a murder mystery so exciting is that it invites the reader or viewer to solve the mystery even before the detective is able to do so.

The religious (biblical, theological, and liturgical) use

> *"Mystery" implies something is hidden.*

of the term is similar to its popular usage, yet different. The similarity lies in the fact that in both instances the word "mystery" implies that something is hidden or is unknown. The difference is twofold: first in popular culture we are invited to figure it out ourselves, while in the religious use of the term the truth is revealed to us not as the result of our successful breaking of the code but rather as a gift bestowed upon us. Second, in popular usage once the puzzle has been solved there is nothing more to be discovered, while in religious usage the mystery is never completely revealed.

In the Catholic Church, we use the religious understanding of the term "mystery" when we refer to God, God's divine plan for us, the sacraments as well as the Church itself.

LOVE in Action

- *What do you think of most immediately when you hear the word "mystery?"*

- *Do the differences between our popular and religious understanding of mystery make sense to you? Explain.*

The Divine Mystery

In the Septuagint, the Greek version of the Bible, the word *mysterion* is used to translate a number of different Hebrew concepts. To give just three examples: in Sirach 27:16, *mysterion* is used to refer to a simple secret: "Whoever betrays a secret [*mysterion*] destroys a confidence, and will never find a congenial friend." Second, *mysterion* is used in reference to a secret (military) plan such as in Judith 2:2: "He summoned all his attendants and officers, laid before them his secret plan [*mysterion*], and with his own lips recounted in full detail the wickedness of all the land." Third, and most importantly, *mysterion* is used to refer to God's secret plan. This can be found, for example, in the Book of Daniel, chapter 2 in the context of Nebuchadnezzar's dream. In this instance, *mysterion* is used to refer to the secret plan that God has for humankind. This secret plan or *mysterion* was revealed by the prophet Daniel as he interpreted Nebuchadnezzar's dream. It is important to note that even though Daniel interpreted the dream and thus revealed the divine mystery or plan, some aspects of it remained unknown and secret.

The usage of the word "mystery" by the Church is similar to the one we find in the biblical usage of *mysterion* in the Book of Daniel. The divine mystery or God's plan for our salvation was at first unknown. Gradually it has been revealed to us, starting in the Old Testament, but most especially in its realization through the mystery of the Incarnation and the paschal mystery. The divine mystery continues to be revealed to us in and through the Church. We know, however, that we will never comprehend the divine mystery totally until all is revealed when we see God face to face at the end of time.

In addition to the divine plan for salvation, God himself is a mystery. Better yet, God is mystery itself. This means that God is essentially unknown and cannot be "researched." Our knowledge of God is dependent upon his self-revelation to us. Examples of this can be found throughout the Bible, for example, when God spoke to Moses in the burning bush (Exodus 3) or to Elijah in the gentle and quiet whisper (1 Kings 19:11–14). God's supreme self-revelation happened in the life, death, and resurrection of his Son Jesus Christ. By extension, God is also revealed in the sacraments or through the Church. Each of these instances gives us a glimpse into who God is, without ever completely revealing the complete mystery of God. The best way to relate to God then is not through our mind, but rather through our heart, since we can never comprehend God completely, but we can love God most deeply.

> *The divine mystery continues to be revealed to us in and through the Church.*

LOVE in Action

- *How would you describe the divine mystery?*
- *Are there biblical images that come to mind when you think of the mystery of God or God revealing himself to one or more people?*
- *How do you relate to God? When you pray how do you address God?*

Mystery of the Incarnation and the Paschal Mystery

The mystery of the Incarnation and the paschal mystery are the two anchors of the divine mystery or God's plan of salvation for us all.

The mystery of the Incarnation essentially is the fact that God adopted our human nature in Jesus. The word "incarnation" is derived from the Latin *carnis,* meaning flesh. Another word for incarnation might be "enfleshment" or the taking on of the human form. Over the past 2,000 years, many aspects of this mystery have been revealed to us. Thus we know that the baby born to the Virgin Mary is indeed the Son of God who became human so he might open for us the way to salvation. Not all has been revealed, though, and some aspects of the Incarnation remain a mystery.

The paschal mystery, the second anchor of our faith, in essence is the mystery of the suffering, death, and resurrection of Jesus Christ. The word "paschal" is derived from the Greek *Pascha,* which in turn is a translation of the Hebrew *Pesah,* meaning Passover. In Judaism, Passover is the celebration of the transition of the Israelites from slavery in Egypt to freedom in the Promised Land. By the grace of God, the Israelites were freed from bondage and death so they might enjoy freedom and life.

Christians see this deliverance from slavery to freedom as a pre-figuration of the ultimate deliverance Jesus won for us through the paschal mystery of his suffering, death, and resurrection. The Christian Passover, or Easter, then celebrates the victory Jesus won over death through his willingness to die on the cross. His victorious death was the ultimate consequence of his radical love for God's people which flowed from his undying love for the Father. Through his death and resurrection Jesus broke the bondage of death and opened the gates to eternal life for all. This in essence is the divine mystery or the mystery of our salvation.

The way humans participate in this salvific sacrifice of Jesus is through the sacraments. Through the sacraments of initiation, Christians are incorporated into the paschal mystery as they die with Christ in order to rise with him again.

The Sacraments— Entering Sacred Mysteries

As baptized Christians, the divine mystery of salvation is not only revealed to us, we also are incorporated in it and benefit from it through the sacraments of initiation: baptism, confirmation, and Eucharist. Thus the sacraments become our gateway into the mystery of salvation and our entrance into the Church.

In the Vulgate, the Latin translation of the Bible uses the Latin word *sacramentum* to translate *mysterion.* Thus *sacramentum* does not only refer to the sacraments or the sacred mysteries but far beyond that to the divine mystery itself.

The root of the word "sacrament" is *sacer,* meaning sacred. Thus through the sacraments, which are our sacred rites, we are incorporated into the sacred mysteries. The Latin fathers chose the word *sacramentum* as translation for *mysterion* based on its military usage. A *sacramentum* in the Roman Empire was a sacred bond between a soldier and his superior which was sealed through an oath and a branding. Similarly, through the sacraments of initiation we enter into a sacred bond with God through the words that are spoken and the sacred signs that are used.

LOVE in Action

- *Which is your favorite: Christmas or Easter? Why?*

- *How do you celebrate Christmas? How do you celebrate Easter?*

- *Can you think of an experience in your life that both has an oath and a sign, thus making some kind of sacramentum?*

- *Do you recall your initiation into the Church? Or maybe you witnessed a baptism? What did you think or feel at the time?*

Mystery of the Church Revealed in Dialogue With World Cultures

The first chapter of the Dogmatic Constitution on the Church (*Lumen Gentium*) promulgated by Vatican II holds that the divine mystery of salvation is present in the Church because in it and through it Christ is present, thus assuring the efficacy of the sacraments. The Church thus is mystery because it shares in the divine mystery and because through it Christians participate in the divine mystery.

An invitation to share in the mystery of salvation through membership in the mystery of the Church has been issued by Catholic missionaries from the start. Successful missionaries have effectively used the idioms and language of the people to whom they have been sent. Saint Paul is a great example of such successful preaching. Not only did he use words and idioms that were familiar to the Greeks, he also used the local media as he proclaimed the Gospel from the *areopagus*, the speaker's corner in Athens during his time.

The success of the Church throughout the ages has been connected with the level of willingness we have had to learn about the people we were preaching to and our willingness to preach the Good News in their own language. The failed attempt at spreading the Gospel in China was greatly due to our unwillingness to adopt some of China's theological language and our refusal to embrace their sensitivity for their ancestors. On the other hand, we have had great success in central Africa because we were willing and able to present our liturgy in the vocabulary of the African people, including African instrumentation, music, and dance.

The mystery of the Church is best revealed when we understand the culture we are communicating with and when we are willing to use the vernacular of any place and time, without abandoning or diluting the Gospel message itself. At the opening of the Second Vatican Council, Blessed Pope John XXIII said we need to "study afresh" and "reformulate in contemporary terms" the "immutable doctrine of our faith" if we want "our doctrine to be more widely known, more deeply understood and more penetrating in its effect." This was not only an invitation to the bishops fifty years ago, it is an invitation to all of us today.

> We need to "reformulate in contemporary terms" the "immutable doctrine of our faith."
> POPE JOHN XXIII

The Mystery of Unity Within Diversity

The reformulation of the truths of the divine mystery in dialogue with our culture was spoken about by Blessed Pope John XXIII as one that necessarily implies an openness to a certain level of diversity, while preserving the shared essence of the faith.

Some people would have us believe that Jesus himself presented us with the Bible, *the Roman Missal,* and the *Catechism of the Catholic Church*. Granted, we do believe that the Scriptures are divinely inspired and that both our liturgy and our doctrine have evolved under the guidance of the Holy Spirit. However, we need to remember that our theology, our liturgy, and even our understanding evolved over time.

In the earliest centuries of the Church, different theologies, different liturgies, and different books of the Bible were used in different parts of the Christian world. Yet the different communities were united in the divine mystery and respected the diversity in which they worshiped and shared the Good News. Even today we have remnants of this great example of unity in diversity as some of the ancient liturgical rites (for example, the Milanese Rite, the Maronite Rite, etc.) have survived and are recognized by the Catholic Church as equal to the Roman Rite.

If we truly believe that the divine mystery of God is gradually revealed to us in time and space, then it follows that the Church—while remaining one, true, and Catholic—continues to evolve. It also follows that as we preach to an increasingly diverse and complex world, the celebration of the mystery of God will become ever richer in diversity. All this, while Christ as the head of his mystical body, the Church holds us all together until at the end of time we will all be perfected in him.

LOVE in Action

- *How do you think the Church can best spread the Gospel in our world?*

- *What do you think are the contributions of Vatican II to the Church and the world?*

- *Are you familiar with some of the different ways in which the Catholic Church celebrates Mass?*

- *Do you believe that we can be one Church but with many different liturgical expressions?*

Concluding Prayer: Ever-living God, Creator of all that is, in your goodness you have given us the gift of your Son as our paschal mystery. Through his death and resurrection, light has destroyed darkness and life has triumphed over death. Through our baptism you have adopted us as your sons and daughters and made us participants in his death and resurrection. Inspire us to more fully acknowledge your tremendous gift, let us live our lives more worthy of this gift, and send us out into the world to testify more vigorously to this gift. We ask this through our Lord Jesus Christ, your Son, our Passover and our hope, who lives with you in the unity of the Holy Spirit, one God forever and ever. Amen.

SUGGESTED RESOURCES

Craghan, John F. *Precious Gifts: Biblical Reflections on the Eucharist* (Liguori Publications, 2011).

Fragomeni, Richard. *The Eucharist: 50 Questions From the Pews* (Liguori Publications, 2008).

Lukefahr, Oscar CM. *We Worship: A Guide to the Catholic Mass* (Liguori Publications, 2004).

Martos, Joseph. *Doors to the Sacred* (Liguori Publications, 2001).

Rolheiser, Ronald. *The Holy Longing: The Search for a Christian Spirituality* (Doubleday Religion, 1999).

Van Parys, Johan PhD. *Symbols That Surround Us: Faithful Reflections* (Liguori Publications, 2012).

Wilkes, Paul. *Holding God in My Hands* (Liguori Publications, 2010).

CINEMA CONNECTION

The Mission (1986), starring Robert De Niro, Jeremy Irons, Ray McAnally. Spanish Jesuits attempt to keep a South American Indian tribe from falling under the rule of proslavery Portugal (set in the eighteenth century).

Steel Magnolias (1989), starring Sally Field, Shirley MacLaine, Dolly Parton, Olympia Dukakis, Daryl Hannah, Julia Roberts. Friendship is a gift that these six "steel magnolias" receive through their life struggles. Laughter and tears are found together in their remarkable stories of love and loss.

ABOUT THE AUTHOR

Johan van Parys, PhD, is the director of liturgy and sacred arts at the Basilica of Saint Mary in Minneapolis. He also teaches liturgy in the School of Theology of St. John's University and is the co-founder and president of the Minnesota/North Dakota Chapter of the Patrons of the Arts in the Vatican Museums. Van Parys received his doctorate in theology in liturgical studies from the University of Notre Dame and has graduate degrees from the Catholic University of Louvain, Belgium, in archeology, art history, architecture, and religious studies.

Notes

SESSION

2

The Church: Ever Ancient, Ever New

By Fr. Mathew J. Kessler, CSsR

Preparation

Have ready a Bible, a candle, matches, and a cross or Christian icon. Set these up on a small table in front of the room where the group will meet, or in the center if you are using a circle format.

Optional

Prepare some simple refreshments for the group to share either before or after the session.

Have music playing quietly in the background on a CD or iPod as participants arrive and settle in.

Opening *TEN MINUTES*

When everyone is seated, light the candle. Begin with the suggested opening song or use one of your choosing. Or you can go directly to the opening prayer found in the session and have everyone read it aloud together.

Scripture Reading

1 Thessalonians 5:12–22

Ask a member of the group to read, or you may read it aloud to the group. Once the passage is read, direct the group to silently reflect for a minute or two on what they have just heard. This also serves as a centering and quieting exercise for participants.

Supporting catechism quotes for Session Two

"The Church, 'the pillar and bulwark of the truth,' faithfully guards 'the faith which was once for all delivered to the saints.' She guards the memory of Christ's words; it is she who from generation to generation hands on the apostles' confession of faith" (CCC 171); see I Timothy 3:15; Jude 3.

"Having been divinely sent to the nations that she might be 'the universal sacrament of salvation,' the Church, in obedience to the command of her founder and because it is demanded by her own essential universality, strives to preach the Gospel to all..." (CCC 849); AG 1; see Matthew 16:15.

"Within the communion of the Church, the Holy Spirit 'distributes special graces among the faithful of every rank' for the building up of the Church. Now, 'to each is given the manifestation of the Spirit for the common good'" (CCC 951); LG 12 #2; 1 Corinthians 12:7.

The Church: Ever Ancient, Ever New

ALLOW FIFTEEN MINUTES FOR EACH SECTION.

Take a few minutes for the group to read through the section, then move to the **LOVE in Action** questions. Allow each person a minute or two to contribute, and give each group member the opportunity to speak.

Additional questions for reflection and discussion

- *Does thinking about the Church as "ever ancient, ever new" generate hope within you? How are you challenged by this phrase?*

- *What pieces of tradition are unchangeable/doctrinal? What traditions are customary? Are there any new traditions that your faith community has enacted? What are some family traditions that have helped you to develop a keener sense of the Gospel message?*

- *List or name some social teachings that the Church has given to the modern world. Might you read an encyclical written by the popes (Rerum Novarum, Pacem in Terris)?*

- *How has the Church gifted you with its message? Consider some ways to further the mission of the Church in your own life.*

Closing Rite

FIVE MINUTES

Invite participants to take part in a few moments of silence, then conclude the lesson by praying the *Prayer of Redemption*:

God of all creation, you rebuild what is broken and restore what has fallen into disrepair. Take our lives into your hands. Breathe your Holy Spirit into us. Restore us to yourself. Make us new and keep us as your own. Amen.

Ask the participants for spontaneous prayer.

When finished, you can offer this brief blessing to the group:

The LORD bless you and keep you!

The LORD let his face shine upon you, and be gracious to you!

The LORD look upon you kindly and give you peace! (Numbers 6: 24–26)

Concluding Prayer: Archbishop Oscar Romero Prayer: *A Step Along The Way*

It helps, now and then, to step back and take a long view. The kingdom is not only beyond our efforts, it is even beyond our vision. We accomplish in our lifetime only a tiny fraction of the magnificent enterprise that is God's work. Nothing we do is complete, which is another way of saying that the Kingdom always lies beyond us. No statement says all that could be said. No prayer fully expresses our faith. No confession brings perfection. No pastoral visit brings wholeness. No program accomplishes the Church's mission. No set of goals and objectives includes everything. This is what we are about. We plant the seeds that one day will grow. We water seeds already planted, knowing that they hold future promise. We lay foundations that will need further development. We provide yeast that produces effects beyond our capabilities. We cannot do everything, and there is a sense of liberation in realizing that. This enables us to do something, and to do it very well. It may be incomplete, but it is a beginning, a step along the way, an opportunity for the Lord's grace to enter and do the rest. We may never see the end results, but that is the difference between the master builder and the worker. We are workers, not master builders; ministers, not messiahs. We are prophets of a future not our own. Amen.

(Composed by Bishop Ken Untener)

SESSION 2

The Church: Ever Ancient, Ever New

By Fr. Mathew J. Kessler, CSsR

WHO embodies the Church?

WHAT challenges face the people of God today?

WHERE might the people of God construct new ways to impart Christ's light on the world?

WHEN does the Church exercise its teaching office?

WHY do we need the teaching office of the Church?

Opening Song: "Anthem," by Tom Conry, or a hymn of your choice

Opening Prayer: Almighty and ever-loving God, we thank you for the gift of the Church. May you enlighten our hearts during this session to hear your word and become more faithful to it. Help us to understand the challenges that face us in the Church today and to work for love, justice, and peace in our communities as laborers in your vineyard. We ask these things through Jesus Christ, our Lord. Amen.

Reading: 1 Thessalonians 5:12–22 (Church order)

Spend a moment in quiet reflection.

Change

A bride-to-be fearing commitment, a parish in a neighborhood undergoing gentrification, an employee being asked to relocate abroad, an aging mother asking her children for help, a father struggling with his daughter's disclosure that she is lesbian, and anyone else whose life is in flux have one thing in common: the rising anxiety they feel as they wonder how their lives are going to change.

To navigate change is to decide what is core to life and what isn't, to distinguish between what we can't let go of and what we can. This is as true of organizations as of people: In each era, the Church must examine the current challenges of the people of God and provide answers through its teaching, preaching, and blessing. For example, the dynamic world economy has caused a shift in the distribution and control of wealth. In rec-

ognizing the Church's responsibility to speak to that shift, the Second Vatican Council expanded Catholic understanding of how the Church should understand and practice justice in contemporary conditions.

As the Church embraces the challenge to decide what is and isn't core to its life, it incorporates new experiences, technologies, and tentative insights into faith tradition and liturgical practice. This makes for a Church that is "ever ancient, ever new."

LOVE in Action

- *What's happening in your parish or community's life today that you didn't expect to ever have to deal with?*

- *How have you adapted to this situation, and what did your community have to learn or do differently because of it?*

New Pastor
New ways

Where Has the Church Changed?

To say the Church has changed generates strong reaction. Change implies imperfection; therefore, some believers contend that to change the Church is to deny its divine source, which is perfection itself. Others note that it's the structures and elements of the Church that are imperfect and need to be adapted.

Is the Church imperfect? Yes. Is the Church divinely inspired? Yes, for Christ promised to accompany the Church with the aid of the Holy Spirit until the end of time. But as John XXIII said in his opening speech at Vatican II (October 11, 1962), the ways in which the truths of the faith are communicated must be examined as well as the condition in which the Church is announcing its message:

> In order, however, that this doctrine may influence the numerous fields of human activity, with reference to individuals, to families, and to social life, it is necessary first of all that the Church should never depart from the sacred patrimony of truth received from the Fathers. But at the same time she must ever look to the present, to the new conditions and new forms of life introduced into the modern world, which have opened new avenues to the Catholic apostolate.

Change brings with it deep personal challenges. (Think about getting the news that your parish church is to close and merge with another parish.) When we're confronted with challenges to careers, political affiliations, and religious practices and beliefs, we respond in one of two ways: fight or flight. Yet the spiritual masters tell us that it's in precisely these times that the spiritual life deepens, that mature people grow through these moments. We become more virtuous and more Christlike as we learn to respond in ways that deepen understanding and build commitment to practicing respect and justice and reconciliation.

Mature Christians carry Tradition forward, giving it new emphasis as we find ourselves in new situations. The term "development of doctrine" describes core Catholic beliefs revealed by God. Because Jesus brought salvation to the world once and for all, the deposit of faith is whole—we can't add to Jesus' revelation.

However, not everything the Church speaks on is doctrinal; certain cultural practices and customs harmonize well with a Catholic vision of life and allow the gospel to be preached more effectively. Catholicism isn't a cult. Catholics don't turn inward and reject the rest of the world, nor do we see the rest of the world as a place where evil reigns and therefore we best not engage it. On the contrary, Jesus' message to the disciples was to go forth, teach, and baptize, to engage the world and bless it. The challenge is to live "in the middle"—in the tension—as Christians fully engaged in and aware of the world. Our message and witness have integrity only when we raise human dignity and announce the Good News of salvation in response to anxious questions.

As the Church responded again and again to the pressing matters of the day, its mission of bringing the Good News to the world through teaching, preaching, and blessing slowly developed.

Teaching

The early Church believed that Jesus was the Son of God and that he was born fully human, but it wasn't until 300 years into its life that the Church found a way to use philosophy to explain this theological truth. An Ecumenical Council at Nicaea in the year 325 made it official, and the doctrine that Jesus was fully human and fully divine is part of the deposit of faith. Through decades—even centuries—this deposit of faith has been explored and, with the help of precise language, a fuller understanding of the doctrine of Jesus' full humanity and divinity has been expressed.

Beliefs we've held for a very long time are made more explicit when theologians, bishops, and the people of God use accurate terminology to explain them. In the early Church, disagreements over a teaching led to polarization and fragmentation of the Church into different sects. Disunity over core beliefs threatened the

Church's witness, and it was essential that the Church address the issue and restore unity.

The Nicene Creed is the Church's liturgical profession of what we believe as Christians. There are other beliefs that aren't contained in the Creed (for example, purgatory), and there are Church practices (called *disciplines*) and devotions that flow from a Catholic vision of life but that are not divinely revealed (for example, the Way of the Cross and vows of poverty, chastity, and obedience).

As Catholics embrace the hard work of understanding these distinctions and transmitting the ancient truths, charity remains a core virtue. (People become passionate and react strongly when core beliefs are challenged.) Blessed John XXIII counsels us with the following wisdom from his first encyclical, On Truth, Unity and Peace, in a Spirit of Charity (*Ad Petri Cathedram*; June 1959):

> But the common saying, expressed in various ways and attributed to various authors, must be recalled with approval: in essentials, unity; in doubtful matters, liberty; in all things, charity (72).

Preaching

In 1891 Pope Leo XIII published his encyclical On Capital and Labor (*Rerum Novarum*), in which he championed the equality of the poor and the wealthy and critiqued the conditions and means by which the poor remained enslaved. While this encyclical was directed toward the conditions of his time, and Leo paid attention to harmony among the classes, the tone and direction of this encyclical cannot be underestimated. The Church was beginning to confront questions and matters of the modern world.

Vatican II (1962–1965) participants continued this tradition in their reflections on the needs of modern people, questioning how government, science, and business affected human life and its dignity. In 1963 Blessed John XXIII released his encyclical On Establishing Universal Peace in Truth, Justice, Charity, and Liberty (*Pacem in Terris*), in which he acknowledged that a new consciousness was astir. He was moved by one of the most important proclamations regarding human dignity of the twentieth century, *The Universal Declaration of Human Rights,* which was promulgated by the United Nations in 1948. That document linked human dignity with associated rights that cannot be violated by another person or institution. The council's continued study of the relationship of the individual to the state—particularly in Communist countries in which believers were punished for practicing their faith—resulted in its 1965 Declaration on Religious Freedom (*Dignitatis Humanae*), a nuanced teaching that all men and women have inherent dignity because they are made in God's image and likeness and endowed with will and rational intellect. That document affirms that no one can be forced to profess a religion.

The dangers and opportunities that exist through new technologies such as stem-cell research, nuclear technology, and globalization require a thoughtful response from the Church. And the faith can continue to guide us, even if it doesn't provide exact answers to such dilemmas. If the Church's voice invites people to conversion and forms consciences in place of moralizing, then it needs to show it understands their anxious questions and complex situations. We are called to be faithful by wrestling with the mysteries of God in our everyday lives. Learning to love under these circumstances demands something that many believers are not comfortable with—ambiguity.

Just as parents must have patience while raising their children by allowing time for discipline, experience, and education to comingle in young lives, so we also need to embrace the ambiguity when a response is not obvious. What happens when we're called to respond, but it's not so clear how to respond? For example, what do we tell a young couple who can't conceive and are thinking about using artificial insemination? What should a pastor or deacon preach on Sunday morning when it's clear that attendance has dropped and there's a need for ministry to a younger, non-Anglo population? Does a bishop minister effectively to all people in his diocese when he decides to close parishes on the basis of financial and personnel resources?

What is the role of the Church—specifically, the minister—in these cases? To teach? To accompany? Many would say both. The challenge is that of leadership, and leadership is about vision and using reason and emotive language to illustrate why change is necessary or why the desired action isn't the most prudent. Loving the Church and one another today requires us to know when to apply principles that form and shape the entire person to be a fully human and fully alive. This calls for fortitude (overcoming the internal forces that prevent us from growing) and courage (overcoming the external forces that prevent us from doing what's right).

Blessing

The sacraments are encounters with Christ. And while they're rooted in the words and mission of Jesus, the structure of sacramental rituals has evolved. Take for example, marriage. You'll look a long time in the Bible for a passage that draws a clear line from the Bible to our Catholic understanding and definition of the sacrament of marriage. This is not to say that biblical tradition doesn't offer words and images about the spiritual significance of marriage; indeed, the people of Israel had laws and customs that regulated marriage as a civil union blessed by God. Jesus was born into a world with this understanding of marriage.

But through Jesus' life, death, and resurrection, marriage became a witness of fidelity to a relationship that promotes love and life. Man and woman become one and pledge to share their gains and losses, joys and sorrows; in their unity is the strength and stability that make a new future possible. A husband and wife reflect commitment in their giving and receiving of vows, just as God chose the people of Israel and each member of the Church.

The more radical take on the sacrament of marriage is the equality of man and woman before God. No one can dispute that for centuries wives were not only oppressed and subject to abuse, but such behaviors were (and continue to be) permitted under some laws. Did the elevation of marriage to a sacrament begin the slow work of consciousness-raising? Did the belief that woman is made in God's image and likeness help challenge social norms that kept women from being true partners in the work of sanctifying daily life?

In this example of the Church developing a sacrament of marriage, one discovers that God's creation has not fulfilled its potential. From the beginning of creation, it was a desire of the Lord that man and woman be equals. Living into this awareness stretches both genders in learning to love under many conditions. There is a kind of humility as the use of money, time, and talents is conditioned by the command to love. In recognizing marriage as a sacrament in the thirteenth century, the Church placed the need for mutual respect and mutual purpose not only on the couple, but on itself as it uses the goods available to it in its mission to announce the kingdom of God.

LOVE in Action

- *How is the Church equipped to deal with new circumstances?*
- *What connections might we draw between a virtuous life and reading the "signs of the times?"*

How Have These Changes Happened?

The developments covered in this chapter have always taken place within the context of community. Individuals may have championed certain points or drafted statements for review, but the wider community has always been involved when core matters are at stake. Church councils give leadership the time and forum to assemble and discern matters of the faith, promote renewal, and address doctrinal questions. The first Church council held in Jerusalem, for example, debated whether uncircumcised Gentiles could be baptized.

When pastoral or doctrinal matters require explanation, bishops fulfill their teaching duties, wisely drawing on the skills of professional theologians in examining matters of the faith and morals. Diocesan synods are a means whereby the people of God give input into matters that affect the vitality of the Catholic faith in their area.

All of these are agents helping the Church keep abreast of matters that affect the faith and its witness in word and deed.

Jesus' command to the apostles to go forth and teach and baptize lives in the Church today. The Church by its nature is missionary. What it has received, it shares with others; its members are a leaven in the world that witnesses to eternal values. We might step back and ask, "Are we much better off after 2,000 years?" An honest response might be, "Yes, but there's work for us to do today." The inspiration for this ongoing work comes from a source beyond human ken, the Holy Spirit, which is at work in the Church, calling it to greater renewal:

It is not only through the sacraments and the ministries of the Church that the Holy Spirit sanctifies and leads the people of God and enriches it with virtues, but, "allotting his gifts to everyone according as He wills." (1 Corinthians 12:11) He distributes special graces among the faithful of every rank. By these gifts He makes them fit and ready to undertake the various tasks and offices which contribute toward the renewal and building up of the Church, according to the words of the apostle: "The manifestation of the Spirit is given to everyone for profit" (1 Thessalonians 5:12, 19–21). These charisms, whether they be the more outstanding or the more simple and widely diffused, are to be received with thanksgiving and consolation for they are perfectly suited to and useful for the needs of the Church (The Dogmatic Constitution on the Church [*Lumen Gentium*], 12).

By no means is the Church always ready with an answer or guidance when pastoral questions surface. The principle to treat others respectfully and with justice is paramount, giving ample time to listen and understand not only what is communicated, but what is meant. In addition, there is value in the spiritual practice of *detachment*, living in proper relationship to those things that aid our spiritual growth and avoiding dependence on goods or convictions that prevent us from growing in the practice of Christian charity.

Learning to love requires first falling in love. To fall in love is to embrace the existence of another person and his or her needs. The gospel exhorts us to lead a full life and describes that life in the language of servanthood. What we receive, we are to pass on through our teaching, preaching, and blessing. Our charge is to undertake this work in ways that are relevant, making a place of comfort and adventure where questions can be expressed and answers found, a place that is "ever ancient and ever new."

LOVE in Action

- *What value is there in having the wider tradition against which to bounce our ideas?*
- *How might institutions contribute to the reign of God or to the injustices of the world? Explain.*
- *How might we bring the message of Jesus into our daily lives? In what ways do we cultivate Christian charity?*

Concluding Prayer:

Archbishop Oscar Romero Prayer: A Step Along The Way

It helps, now and then, to step back and take a long view.

The kingdom is not only beyond our efforts,

      it is even beyond our vision.

We accomplish in our lifetime only a tiny fraction of the magnificent enterprise
      that is God's work.

Nothing we do is complete, which is another way of saying that the Kingdom
      always lies beyond us.

No statement says all that could be said.

No prayer fully expresses our faith.

No confession brings perfection.

No pastoral visit brings wholeness.

No program accomplishes the Church's mission.

No set of goals and objectives includes everything.

This is what we are about.

We plant the seeds that one day will grow.

We water seeds already planted, knowing that they hold future promise.

We lay foundations that will need further development.

We provide yeast that produces effects beyond our capabilities.

We cannot do everything, and there is a sense of liberation in realizing that.

This enables us to do something, and to do it very well.

It may be incomplete, but it is a beginning, a step along the way,
      an opportunity for the Lord's grace to enter and do the rest.

We may never see the end results, but that is the difference between the master builder
      and the worker.

We are workers, not master builders; ministers, not messiahs.

We are prophets of a future not our own. Amen.

COMPOSED BY BISHOP KEN UNTENER

SUGGESTED RESOURCES:

Baum, Gregory. *Amazing Church: A Catholic Theologian Remembers a Half-Century of Change* (Novalis, 2005).

Wright, David F., Sinclair B. Ferguson, and J.I. Packer. *New Dictionary of Theology* (See entries: *Deposit of Faith; Development of Doctrine; Love; Virtue*). [IVP Academic, 1997].

CINEMA CONNECTION

A Man for All Seasons (1966), starring Paul Scofield, Wendy Hiller, Leo McKern. Depicts the story of Saint Thomas More—an English clergyman and lawyer—standing up to the king of England.

ABOUT THE AUTHOR

Fr. Mathew J. Kessler, CSsR, was born in Wichita, Kansas, and graduated from Wichita State University with a degree in physics before beginning studies for the Catholic priesthood. He was granted a master of divinity degree from Catholic Theological Union and ordained in 1991. He served as a parish priest and mission preacher for ten years, largely among the Latino community, before his 2001 appointment as managing editor of Liguori's Spanish imprint, *Libros Liguori*. In 2006, Kessler became president and publisher of Liguori Publications, serving in these roles until 2013. He continues the ministry of sharing the Good News of our plentiful redemption.

Conversion and Spiritual Maturity

By Andrés Arango

Preparation

Have ready a Bible, a candle, matches, and a cross or Christian icon. Set these up on a small table in front of the room where the group will meet, or in the center if you are using a circle format.

Optional

Prepare some simple refreshments for the group to share either before or after the session.

Have music playing quietly in the background on a CD or iPod as participants arrive and settle in.

Opening TEN MINUTES

When everyone is seated, light the candle. Begin with the suggested opening song or use one of your choosing. Or you can go directly to the opening prayer found in the session and have everyone read it aloud together.

Scripture Reading

Matthew 5:43–48

Ask a member of the group to read, or you can read it aloud to the group. Once the passage is read, direct the group to silently reflect for a minute or two on what they have just heard. This also serves as a centering and quieting exercise for participants.

Supporting catechism quotes for Session Three

"The new life received in Christian initiation has not abolished the frailty and weakness of human nature, nor the inclination to sin that tradition calls concupiscence, which remains in the baptized such that with the help of the grace of Christ they may prove themselves in the struggle of Christian life" (see DS 1515). "This is the struggle of conversion directed toward holiness and eternal life to which the Lord never ceases to call us" (CCC 1426); see DS 1545; LG 40.

"Christ's call to conversion continues to resound in the lives of Christians....It is an uninterrupted task for the whole Church. This endeavor of conversion is not just a human work. It is the movement of a 'contrite heart' (Psalm 51:19), drawn and moved by grace (see John 6:44, 12:32) to respond to the merciful love of God who loved us first" (CCC 1428); see 1 John 4:10.

"Conversion requires convincing of sin; it includes the interior judgment of conscience, and this, being a proof of the action of the Spirit of truth in man's inmost being, becomes at the same time the start of a new grant of grace and love: 'Receive the Holy Spirit.' Thus in this 'convincing concerning sin' we discover a double gift: the gift of the truth of conscience and the gift of the certainty of redemption" (CCC 1848); John Paul II, DeV 31 # 2.

Conversion and Spiritual Maturity

ALLOW FIFTEEN MINUTES FOR EACH SECTION.

Take a few minutes for the group to read through the section, then move to the **LOVE in Action** questions. Allow each person a minute or two to contribute, and give each group member the opportunity to speak.

Additional questions for reflection and discussion

- *Conversion is a process that usually involves a radical change at some time in our lives, but that constantly requires us to examine our lives in order to make a daily decision to follow and imitate Jesus. Where are you in the conversion process? Have you made a radical decision in your life to return to the way of Jesus? What do you do daily to be aware of how your life is linked to the Lord Jesus? What spiritual activities do you enact to become more like our Lord?*

- *We all have a general call in our lives—the call to be saints. What does holiness mean to you? Would you feel comfortable with other people calling you a holy person? Why or why not? What are God's expectations of you in order to lead a life of holiness?*

- *There are several stages in our spiritual journey. What stage are you in right now? The purgative, illuminative, or unitive stage? What can you do to continue growing into a greater state of spiritual perfection? What other stages have you heard about from some of the mystics of the Church?*

- *The Holy Spirit is the main person who enables our spiritual growth. How is your relationship with the Holy Spirit? What can you do to let the Spirit act in your life, making your life more likened to Christ Jesus? How can you put the gifts God has given you at the service of others for the good of the community?*

Closing Rite

FIVE MINUTES

Invite participants to take part in a few moments of silence, then ask the participants for spontaneous prayer. You may conclude the session with Psalm 51:3–12 (found in your Bible).

When finished, you can offer this brief blessing to the group:

Oh God! Bless and watch over us while we set out to share your love and the Good News of Jesus Christ with all those we encounter in our daily lives.

Concluding Prayer: Heavenly Father, we thank you because you created us in your image and likeness. Dear Jesus, we praise you with all our hearts for becoming man and coming to reveal your infinite love to us. Thank you, Holy Spirit, for dwelling within us, for providing us with different gifts to help us grow in our spiritual life. Blessed Trinity, we ask you to give us the grace to grow in your love and reflect it to all around us. Amen.

Conversion and Spiritual Maturity

By Andrés Arango

WHO guides us in our spiritual growth?

WHAT does it mean to be in the process of conversion?

WHERE might we find tools to assist our stages of spiritual growth?

WHEN are we called to be saints?

WHY am I invited to live life in the Spirit?

Opening Song: "Psalm 103: The Lord Is Kind and Merciful," by Marty Haugen and David Haas, or a hymn of your choice

Opening Prayer: God our Creator, you have called us to this community known as the Catholic Church. Bless our work during today's session to better understand who we are and where we come from as members of the Church. Open our minds and hearts to your word and the words of those who have gathered today. Inspire us with your Spirit and guide us on the path of Jesus Christ, our Lord. Amen.

Reading: Matthew 5:43–48 (love of enemies)

Spend a moment in quiet reflection.

Conversion

The Old Testament prophets exhorted the people to convert. John the Baptist always mentioned the urgency of conversion in his preaching (Matthew 3:2). And Jesus' public life begins with him preaching conversion: "Repent, for the kingdom of heaven is at hand" (Matthew 4:17).

The word "conversion" comes from the Greek *metanoia*, which could also be translated as "radical change." Many times, a conversion is marked only by a life change in which we drop some vice or stop doing something considered bad. However, conversion goes beyond that. Indeed, the absence of sin can only mean being in the middle of the process and not giving our life the required turnaround.

We can compare the conversion process to the experience of having to travel to a certain place and boarding the wrong plane by mistake. Obviously, since it is the wrong plane, your assigned seat would be occupied, so you would sit in another. Upon realizing the error, you should hurry, get off the plane, and more importantly board the right one. Something similar happens in our lives. We often go where the current of the world takes us, following the path of many others. Despite signs that warn us that we are on the wrong path, we settle in, confident that we're going to the right place. True conversion does not mean simply abandoning the path we undertook, but rather following the only way—Jesus Christ.

Conversion does not only mean sinlessness. It is not just following a specific set of rules that gives us the title of saint or holy. Conversion involves a radical change, setting out on a new path, a path full of forgiveness, mercy, hope, and love. Conversion is the beginning of a relationship with a real and living God; a God who became human and loved us to the end in order to show us that there is indeed true life in him.

In order to enter into a deepened spiritual life and our path of growth in God, we must start with a profound conversion experience. However, this experience is a process that never ends. Each of us remembers an event or a particular stage of our life which marked a radical and significant change. But beyond that, conversion is part of a cycle that we human beings live through, a cycle that involves failures and falls, but also repentance and rising again in the arms of God, who guides our journey onto the right path. Every day we face situations of conversion, moments that involve taking a real radical decision that channels our journey toward God.

> *Conversion means following Jesus Christ.*

LOVE in Action

- *Think for a moment about how you are living your daily conversion process. What things do you still need to completely surrender to the Lord?*

- *What might we do today to take another step on the road to a complete configuration with Jesus?*

- *Before making an important decision today, think about how you can make a radical decision so that your way is God's way.*

God's Plan for Humanity

We were created in the image and likeness of God in order to reflect God's face, convey his love, share his peace, and especially to have complete happiness. God has a plan, a mission for each of us. However, no matter what our vocation, our profession, or our state of life, we all have a special calling to holiness. So in summary, God's plan for all human beings is for us to be saints. But is it really possible to be holy? Do we have the capacity to achieve that ideal?

First, we must define what holiness is. Holiness is to be called apart or chosen. Unfortunately, many of the images we have of the saints in the temples reflect suffering, or sad, withdrawn faces; yet all the men and women throughout history who have walked the path of holiness have been filled with joy and happiness. No saint is or was without joy. Lately there have been different portraits of the smiling Jesus, a new wave of Christian art that depicts Jesus playing, laughing, and full of joy. I think it's something that shows us a reality that is closer to holiness. For this presents an image of the God who knew how to live every moment of his earthly life by sharing his infinite love.

Bishop Alfonso Uribe Jaramillo, a great Colombian bishop, gives us an anecdotal but very profound definition of holiness that was uttered by a child looking at the windows of a great cathedral on the day he made his first Communion: "A saint is someone who lets in sunlight." Holiness is a gift from God. The Holy Spirit's mission is to sanctify, or rather, to make us holy men and women. Our duty is to open ourselves to the action of the divine Spirit, who began to dwell in us at our baptisms. But in order to stir the fire of the Spirit who fills our lives, we must be sincere and clear like the stained glass windows of a cathedral. For the Spirit living in us will bring light and warmth to all God's people.

Thus holiness is not just a fulfillment of rules. It goes beyond that, for it involves a lifestyle to be lived at all times. It means having the thoughts and feelings of Jesus. In other words, it is a lifestyle that leads us to be like Jesus.

Spiritual Growth and Life Stages

We are all called to be like Jesus, that is, to be saints. But our growing into his likeness will depend on each of our particular callings, vocations, and states of life. According to the *Aparecida Document*, the bishops are called to be like Jesus the priest; priests are called to be like Jesus the shepherd; deacons are called to be like Jesus the servant; consecrated souls are called to be witnesses to Jesus; and the laity are called to be the light of the world. Each of us must reflect these aspects of Jesus, but in specific ways according to our states of life.

There are various vocations, ministries, and calls, including vocations that arise in our adulthood. However, individually we are all called to grow in our spiritual lives and be increasingly conformed to Jesus in the different stages of our lives.

LOVE in Action

- *Think for a moment about how you are living your call to holiness each day. What can you do today to really be recognized as a person with a holy life?*

- *What kind of lifestyle did Jesus have during his earthly life? Evaluate your lifestyle. What might you do to make your lifestyle more like Jesus'?*

- *Think about the particular vocation to which God has called you. What can you do today to reflect a particular quality of Jesus according to your state of life?*

The Stages of Spiritual Growth

Over the centuries, various Christian authors have described paths of spiritual life based on different stages. Saint Teresa of Ávila described the path like a house of seven mansions; Thomas Merton describes it through his biography and the various states he went through. For Merton indicated discovering God is initiated by delving into ourselves. Here we rely on three basic steps that will help us identify what state we are in and how we can keep climbing each one.

Purgative Stage

The initial step for those who have opened their hearts to God's action and have decided to launch and grow in their relationship with the Lord is usually called "purgative." It is usually characterized by great consolations, as Saint Ignatius of Loyola described them in the sixteenth century. We can compare such consolations to a "honeymoon" in which God gives us sweets to follow and fall in love with him. It is accompanied with a state of peace and spiritual joy.

At the same time, this step includes major purifications, especially of the person's vices and sins. Also, there is a purification of the senses that helps us overcome the attraction of things that are not according to God's will. Many times God removes the consolations and a passive purification begins. It is said that this is to teach a person to go beyond simply feeling the pleasures of prayer and to help him or her desire a deeper relationship with Christ.

The purgative stage is usually associated with forms of prayer that are primarily focused on sin and its consequences: death, judgment, heaven, hell, that is, the last things. Here people really begin to seek not their own will, but they desire to do God's will more and more in their lives.

There are two forms of purification in this stage: active and passive. In the active form of purification, the soul performs voluntary mortifications, sacrifices, works, and sufferings. In the passive form of purification, God acts to deliver the person from bondage to vice and sin. In this stage, there are events, circumstances, and happenings that lead the person to spiritual growth. It is in this stage that we see great conversions and hear the tremendous testimonies of souls touched by the love and grace of God.

Discovering God, says Thomas Merton, involves delving into ourselves.

Illuminative Stage

During this stage, the person makes great spiritual progress, avoiding all mortal sin and attachment to the world. It is called "illuminative" because here the converted mind and heart are becoming more enlightened with the practice of virtues and filled with a greater desire to reach complete union with Christ.

This stage is characterized by an increase in the experience of the central Christian virtue: charity. The person multiplies his works of charity and commitment to the neediest. People in this stage begin not only to think less about themselves, but to see the importance of their commitment to serving others.

The prayer that is most often associated with this stage is meditation (*Catechism of the Catholic Church* 2705). People in this stage regularly meditate on the mysteries of the life of Jesus through the rosary and attend silent retreats. They read and meditate more on sacred Scripture, particularly through the *Liturgy of the Hours* and *Lectio Divina*. In turn, they begin to desire more silence during prayer. The consistency between their life of prayer and action increases. That is, they do not only talk about God but reflect his presence through the witness of their lives. As Pope Paul VI said in *Evangelii Nuntiandi*: "Modern man listens more willingly to witnesses than to teachers, and if he does listen to teachers, it is because they are witnesses" (No. 41).

The illuminative stage can last for many years after passing through the purgative stage. Often there are a number of great desolations and consolations. Consolations are usually feelings of fervor, joy, and devotion. These often start with the senses but grow with the exercise of virtues based on the intellect and the will. The desolations are usually feelings of being abandoned by God. This can occur because of our bad decisions, malicious attacks, or by God allowing the soul to be purified.

Saint John of the Cross said that at this stage one can occupy the mind in God with much greater ease and joy than in the purgative stage. The person can also encounter purifications, usually characterized by spiritual dryness, boredom, trials, and darkness in prayer (CCC 2729). The person often experiences external suffering caused by persecution by others, betrayals, and significant losses. But through these trials and sufferings, God is with us and is a means by which our faith grows day by day. Perseverance is important at this stage, marked mainly by the feeling of God's abandonment and constant perseverance in our walk.

Unitive Stage

Those in the unitive stage have persevered in absolutely desiring and seeking only God's will. This is the stage of perfection, as Saint Teresa of Jesus describes in the Mansions of the Interior Castle. At this stage the person is practically and completely separated from his ego and from the desire to be praised and recognized. People in this stage have a different perspective and acceptance of the concerns of the world. They have reached a state of great peace, despite the trials they confront every day. And they possess that peace that Jesus speaks about in the Gospel, a peace that only he can give us (John 14:27); a peace that does not depend on earthly things and that is not disturbed by them, but instead is firm and unchanging, sustained by trust and abandonment to God.

This is also known as the stage of perfect charity, because people have great empathy with others, particularly with everyone they meet in their daily lives. And their life, thus, becomes completely geared toward service.

This stage is known as unitive because the soul is united to God with bonds of pure and selfless love. The soul is willing to give love without receiving anything in return, a love like the one Saint Paul refers to in his Letter to the Corinthians (1 Corinthians 13). Love is not only based on feelings, but on a real decision, as Emeritus Pope Benedict XVI exhorts in the encyclical God Is Love.

Here, what Saint Paul says is fulfilled: "Whoever is joined to the Lord becomes one spirit with him" (1 Corinthians 6:17). The prayer that is most related to this stage is contemplation (CCC 2709). God speaks to us in a particular way through the life of Jesus, his resurrection, ascension, Pentecost, etc. There is a strong desire not only to talk toward God, but mostly to listen and rejoice in God's presence, in his mystery. Like Mary, the person abandons himself or herself completely in God. One may not understand many things, but offers his or her fiat, a radical "yes" like the Virgin's (Luke 1:38).

Many souls who have reached a very high level of this type of prayer are adorned with mystical experiences and extraordinary gifts of God. However, Saint John of the Cross warns that those who have reached this stage may still be purified as they find crosses and difficulties greater than those they experienced in the purgative and illuminative stages. Therefore, this stage is not always free from trouble or purification.

LOVE in Action

- *Today offer a small sacrifice to God and feel God's presence within you accompanying you as you make an offering of something that you like.*

- *Select the text that you most relate to in the word of God. Read it and then imagine that you are like a character in that passage. What is God revealing to you through the word?*

- *Do something kind (an act of charity) for someone you meet this week.*

God's Continuous Presence—How It Changes Our Lives

Throughout the history of the Church, there have been currents of the so-called super Christians or those who think that by their own efforts they will achieve conformity to Christ. However, we know that spiritual growth is the result of God at work within us. This does not mean we have to have a passive attitude; on the contrary, we are called to open ourselves to the action of the Holy Spirit to work mightily in our lives.

On the day we were baptized, we received great graces and gifts, but the most special of all is that we received the Holy Spirit for the first time. God comes to dwell in us, as Saint Paul says in 1 Corinthians 3:16 and also in Ephesians 4:30. However, this implies an active attitude, allowing the Spirit to move within us and guide us.

The first step in allowing ourselves be led by the third person of the Trinity is to recognize the Spirit's presence within us; in other words, it is to consciously allow the Holy Spirit to act in our lives, making room to enact God's desires for us.

Second, it is important to have a constant relationship with the Holy Spirit, that is, to have a deep prayer life in which we ask every day for the Holy Spirit to maintain an active presence within us. The grand old hymn that says "come, Holy Spirit" remains ever timely, since God is inexhaustible, so we can always receive our Lord in a new way. Also, reading the Scriptures, particularly the Gospels and Acts of the Apostles, gives us an overview of the action of God's Spirit in Jesus, the disciples, and the early Christian communities. Through these models of the spiritual life, we can discern how the Spirit acts and, adapted to our modern world, we see how we can let Spirit lead us to reach our spiritual goal—to be like Jesus.

Third, it is important to ask for the gift of discernment, which helps us distinguish what gifts the Holy Spirit has given us, because when we faithfully use the graces the Spirit gives, God helps us to be faithful to our mission. This also motivates us to build up the body of Christ, since a true spiritual growth is in complete connection to community life.

Finally, the Holy Spirit's gifts are not the most important thing. The key is to bear fruit. The Letter to the Galatians mentions several of these fruits of the Spirit (Galatians 5:22–23). Thus, the presence of God in our lives changes us and takes us through different states in order to truly reflect Jesus.

The Old Testament often connects holiness to rule-following. However, Jesus came to present to us a new way—he shows us the way to love and on the Sermon on the Mount he gave us the Beatitudes. Every day we face different decisions, not merely about choosing between good and evil. There are also circumstances related to the state of our own lives, such as disease and economic situations, that require us to respond as Christ would. In this sense, the Sermon on the Mount provides a way to grow spiritually in order to increasingly resemble our Lord.

Therefore, God is continually at work in our lives. Jesus delivers us with the power of his precious blood from the various ties that bind us to vices and lead us to sin. He heals us from the inner wounds that have marked our lives and that prevent us from being happy. And he heals the fears that do not let us live in the freedom of the children of God. God transforms us completely, changing our minds so that we have the same thoughts as Jesus and our hearts so that we have the mind of Christ. In conclusion, God is working to make us like him.

Echoing the words of Paul, a beautiful song says, "We are citizens of heaven" (from Philippians 3:20). It is important to have an eternal perspective on our lives. The goal of growing spiritually and conforming ourselves to Christ is to prepare for glory. Jesus said he would prepare a celestial abode for us (John 14:2). However much one might try to describe what heaven is like, we will know only when we are there and meet our God face to face. What we can be sure of is that heaven will be the experience of being with God, and if it is possible to speak about time in eternity, heaven

"Come, Holy Spirit" remains ever timely.

will be knowing God in a new way at every instant, falling in love with him at every moment. For God, who is love (1 John 4:7), does not tire—God's love is creative, dynamic, and ever new. The Book of Revelation says: "I make all things new" (Revelation 21:5), so God renews us each day.

If we could summarize Christianity in one word, it would be "LOVE." The goal of the spiritual life is to be filled with the love of God so as to be able to share it with others. That is, to live as Jesus did, being able even to give our lives for others, forgetting ourselves. Therefore, frequently receiving Jesus in the Eucharist, the "source and summit of the whole Christian life" (*LG* 11), is key to being able to progress in our spiritual growth, achieve union with God and Christ. In turn, constantly asking the Holy Spirit to act within us enables us to be guided by the Holy Spirit in order to live like Jesus, filled with the Spirit—in other words, full of the love of God.

LOVE in Action

- *Read the Sermon on the Mount preached by Jesus in the Gospel of Matthew (5:1–12). Resolve to live one of those beatitudes today.*

- *Think about who needs Jesus' light to pass through you. Bring love to the people God puts in your heart.*

- *Regard the gifts the Holy Spirit has given you and put them at the service of God through an activity for your community/parish.*

Concluding Prayer: Heavenly Father, we thank you because you created us in your image and likeness. Dear Jesus, we praise you with all our hearts for becoming man and coming to reveal your infinite love to us. Thank you, Holy Spirit, for dwelling within us, for providing us with different gifts to help us grow in our spiritual life. Blessed Trinity, we ask you to give us the grace to grow in your love and reflect it to all around us. Amen.

SUGGESTED RESOURCES:

Kessler, Mathew J. CSsR, and José Antonio Medina, SDT. *With Hearts Full of Joy: Following Christ the Redeemer* (Liguori Publications, 2010).

McColman, Carl. *The Big Book of Christian Mysticism: The Essential Guide to Contemplative Spirituality* (Hampton Roads Publishing, 2010).

Rohr, Richard. *The Naked Now: Learning to See as the Mystics See* (The Crossroad Publishing Company, 2009).

Rolheiser, Ronald. *The Holy Longing: The Search for a Christian Spirituality* (Doubleday Religion, 1999).

CINEMA CONNECTION

Romero (1989), starring Raul Julia, Richard Jordan, Ana Alicia. The story of Archbishop Oscar Romero and his opposition to repression in El Salvador.

ABOUT THE AUTHOR

Andrés Arango is the bishop's delegate for Hispanic Ministry and the director of evangelization, Office of Lifelong Faith Formation, in the Diocese of Camden (New Jersey). He is also the national coordinator of the Hispanic Catholic Charismatic Renewal in the United States and Canada. Arango serves as a member of the Latin American Catholic Charismatic Council. He has been an active minister, and he authored the book *Con Poder...La Experiencia de Pentecostés* in 2009. Among his educational accomplishments, Arango has a master's degree in theological studies from the Franciscan School of Theology in Berkeley, California. He is a native of Medellín, Colombia.

4

Sacred Scripture: The Story of Salvation

By Pía Septién

Preparation

Have ready a Bible, a candle, matches, and a cross or Christian icon. Set these up on a small table in front of the room where the group will meet, or in the center if you are using a circle format.

Optional

Prepare some simple refreshments for the group to share either before or after the session.

Have music playing quietly in the background on a CD or iPod as participants arrive and settle in.

Opening *TEN MINUTES*

When everyone is seated, light the candle. Begin with the suggested opening song or use one of your choosing. Or you can go directly to the opening prayer found in the session and have everyone read it aloud together.

Scripture Reading

Deuteronomy 11:18–21

Ask a member of the group to read, or you can read it aloud to the group. Once the passage is read, direct the group to silently reflect for a minute or two on what they have just heard. This also serves as a centering and quieting exercise for participants.

Supporting catechism quotes for Session Four

"The Old Testament is an indispensable part of Sacred Scripture. Its books are divinely inspired and retain a permanent value, for the Old Covenant has never been revoked" (CCC 121); see DV 14.

"'The Word of God, which is the power of God for salvation to everyone who has faith, is set forth and displays its power in a most wonderful way in the writings of the New Testament' which hand on the ultimate truth of God's Revelation. Their central object is Jesus Christ, God's incarnate Son: his acts, teachings, Passion and glorification, and his Church's beginnings under the Spirit's guidance" (CCC 124); see DV 15; DV 20.

"The Church, as early as apostolic times (see 1 Corinthians 10:6, 11; Hebrews 10:1; 1 Peter 3:21), and then constantly in her Tradition, has illuminated the unity of the divine plan in the two Testaments through typology, which discerns in God's works of the Old Covenant prefigurations of what he accomplished in the fullness of time in the person of his incarnate Son" (CCC 128).

Sacred Scripture: The Story of Salvation

ALLOW FIFTEEN MINUTES FOR EACH SECTION.

Take a few minutes for the group to read through the section, then move to the **LOVE in Action** questions. Allow each person a minute or two to contribute, and give each group member the opportunity to speak.

Additional questions for reflection and discussion

- *What are some main characteristics of each Gospel?*
- *Why do we say that the Gospels are not a biography of Jesus?*
- *Which of the Gospels was written last?*
- *Why is the Gospel of John very different from the other three?*
- *Who are the recipients of each of the Gospels?*

Closing Rite

FIVE MINUTES

Invite participants to take part in a few moments of silence, then ask the participants for spontaneous prayer. When finished you can offer this brief blessing to the group:

Oh God! Bless and watch over us while we set out to share your love and the Good News of Jesus Christ with all those we encounter in our daily lives.

Concluding Prayer: Lord Jesus, you are the fulfillment of all our hopes and desires. Fill us with the joy of the Gospel and inflame our hearts with love for all our brothers and sisters, humankind. Amen.

Sacred Scripture:
The Story of Salvation

By Pía Septién

WHO is Jesus for Mark?

WHAT are the Gospels?

WHERE do we find the story of Paul's conversion?

WHEN did John write his Gospel?

WHY is the Gospel of Matthew known as the didactic or catechetical Gospel?

Opening Song: "Morning Has Broken," by Cat Stevens, or a hymn of your choice

Opening Prayer: God our Creator, you provided us with your Holy Scripture. We are thankful you have made yourself known to us through the Gospels, the person of Jesus, and all of your holy word. Help us to hear you today and to walk in the footsteps of Jesus our Savior. Guide and inspire us with your Spirit as we seek you this day, dear Lord. Amen.

Reading: Deuteronomy 11:18–21 (God's word)

Spend a moment in quiet reflection.

The Big News

The New Testament tells the greatest story ever told, recounting the life and teachings of Jesus and of the first community of his followers. It consists of twenty-seven books, which were not written in the same era, but were gradually completed over a period of fifty years. The Gospels were written in Greek, since their intended recipients were the different churches formed by Jesus' early followers, who were called Christians.

In this session we will study the four Gospels and the Acts of the Apostles.

What Are the Gospels?

The Gospels are an account of faith that seek to proclaim the living Jesus. They are not a biography nor a narrative intended only to present the story of Jesus. Rather, they are the proclamation of the Good News of Jesus; that is, the Good News that Jesus of Nazareth bore credible witness to humanity by miracles, signs, and wonders that God performed through him when he was among us. He was betrayed and crucified according to God's plan. But God raised him up, breaking the bonds of death (Acts 2:22–25).

Therefore, the Gospels are the fervent proclamation of the Good News: Jesus of Nazareth is the Lord, and he is risen!

In the Scriptures, we find four Gospels: Matthew, Mark, Luke, and John. Each presents a particular account of Jesus, his mission, and his teachings. This makes the story vary according to each evangelist's style. Thus we find that some are longer than others and in some certain words or concepts are repeated. For example, in many of his passages, Luke speaks about prayer; Matthew makes repeated reference to the need to protect the most vulnerable, whom he calls "these little ones."

Despite their differences in diction, the Gospels should be considered as a unified work and not merely as a series of isolated passages. When we read, we need do so with the intention that the authors had at the time of their composition, which was to present an account of the sayings and deeds of Jesus, the Messiah, the Son of God.

The New Testament has been studied through the centuries and has been analyzed by experts; beyond this, it has been the means by which millions of people have encountered the person of Jesus, a great source of hope. Like Jesus and the Samaritan woman, who was thirsting to know and love God (John 4) when she was met by the Lord at the side of the well, so we meet Jesus in the Gospels. And these encounters lead us to approach the God for whom we are thirsting, even at times unknowingly.

The Gospels are the Good News of Jesus and of the freedom he won for us with his passion, death, and resurrection. And this Good News is just as valid today as it was when Jesus walked the earth in the first century. And it will continue to be so in the future, for God's word has the ability to change, transform, release, and heal those who receive the Good News of Jesus, our Lord.

> *The Gospels are the fervent proclamation of the Good News.*

LOVE in Action

- *How well do you know the Gospels? Have you read them all the way through?*
- *According to you, are the Gospels the proclamation of the Good News? If so, what can you do to spread the Good News of Jesus?*

Jesus Is the Master

For many centuries, the Gospel of Matthew was the most quoted Gospel in the Christian tradition and also the most studied. It comes first in order of the canon of the New Testament not because it was the first to be written, since some of the letters of Paul and the Gospel of Mark were written before it, but because it serves as a bridge between the Old and the New Testaments.

The main objective of this Gospel is to convince the followers of Jesus, who were of Jewish origin, that he indeed is the king, the Messiah or Christ, the Anointed One, the Son of God. This Gospel begins with the genealogy of Jesus, which leads us to see how Jesus comes from the house of David, king of Israel; and from Abraham, the Jew *par excellence*.

Matthew seeks to give his fellow Jews necessary evidence so that they too can to come to believe that Jesus is truly the king of the Jews. At the beginning of the Gospel, the Magi attest to his kingship by asking, "Where is the newborn king of the Jews? We saw his star at its rising and have come to do him homage" (2:2). Near the end of the Gospel, Pilate asks Jesus, "Are you the king of the Jews?" (27:11) to which he replies, "You say so." To prove to them that Jesus is indeed the king of the Jews, Matthew quotes extensively from the prophets of the Old Testament, showing how Jesus fulfilled all that had been foretold about the Messiah who would come to establish the kingdom of God.

This is a story that seeks not only to maintain but to increase the faith of a Christian community that came from Judaism. The Christian converts from Judaism were a community that left the stability and security of an ancient religion to follow Jesus as their only Lord. So Matthew wants to make it clear that the old law from the Old Testament would continue to stand: "Do not think that I have come to abolish the law or the prophets. I have come not to abolish but to fulfill" (5:17). He seeks to reaffirm their conviction that Christians are truly the heirs of God's people, and that they are the true recipients of the promises. Therefore, they should not depart from faith in Jesus of Nazareth.

While the evangelist Mark focuses his Gospel on the "events" of Jesus' life and ministry, Matthew focuses on the "teachings" of Jesus. Jesus' teachings about the kingdom of God are organized into five major discourses, which Matthew places before his miracles. Matthew seeks to emphasize that Jesus is the true master, which is why his Gospel is called the didactic or catechetical Gospel. In his Gospel, we find five great discourses, namely: the Sermon on the Mount, on the attitudes that must be kept with respect to the Law (5–7); the choice of the twelve Apostles and his instructions for their apostolic mission, (10); seven parables about the kingdom of heaven (13); life in the community, where he talks about "greatness" and "forgiveness" in the kingdom, (18); and the eschatological discourse, dealing with Jesus' exhortation to hope and watchfulness (24–25).

Matthew's account emphasizes Jesus' divine authority, an authority that comes from being God. He has authority over nature by his miracles, over sin by forgiving it, and over death through his resurrection. He also has power over those men to whom he conferred ministries. He tells Peter, "I will give you the keys of the kingdom of heaven. Whatever you bind on earth shall be bound in heaven; and whatever you loose on earth shall be loosed in heaven" (16:19). Jesus' last words to his apostles before ascending into heaven also speak of this divine authority, as he tells them, "All power in heaven and on earth has been given to me. Go, therefore, and make disciples of all nations, baptizing them in the name of the Father, and of the Son, and of the holy Spirit, teaching them to observe all that I have commanded you. And behold, I am with you always, until the end of the age" (28:18–20).

In conclusion, Matthew's Gospel proclaims that Jesus is the teacher who talks about the kingdom of God and eternal life and teaches that the most important thing is to love God and neighbor.

LOVE in Action

• *At the end of the Gospel of Matthew, Jesus commands the disciples to make disciples of all nations, "teaching them to observe all that I have commanded you." What can you do to get more people to be disciples or followers of Jesus?*

Mark's Gospel: Old, Not Outdated

The Gospel of Mark is the oldest of the Gospels, the first missionary text that presents us with the person and mission of Jesus. The text paints an attractive portrait with plenty of details, for Mark's memories of the life of Jesus were still very fresh at that time.

He begins with the assertion that Jesus is the Christ and the Son of God (1:1). Jesus was not simply a man among others. He was someone who caused astonishment and admiration among those who met him: "the people were astonished" (1:22), "all were amazed" (1:27), "the disciples were amazed at his words" (10:24). This Gospel illumines for us a very human Jesus: "The carpenter, the son of Mary" (6:3), who "sighed from the depth of his spirit" (8:12) and seeing the crowd "his heart was moved with pity for them" (6:34), who in the midst of the storm was able to sleep in the stern on a cushion (4:38).

Mark uses words from the Aramaic, but he translates them so that his foreign readers can understand them. For example: *Abba*: Father (14:36), *Ephphatha*: be opened (7:34) *Eloi, Eloi*: My God, My God (15:34). He explains Jewish customs such as not eating with unwashed hands (7:3–5) and what happens on the feast of unleavened bread (14:12).

Mark presents Jesus in action and with a sense of urgency. He tells us that "when [Jesus] got out of the boat, at once a man from the tombs who had an unclean spirit met him" (5:2), that when he cured a blind man, "immediately he received his sight and followed him on the way" (10:52). When Peter's mother was ill, "He approached, grasped her hand, and helped her up. Then the fever left her" (1:31).

When asked who Jesus is, Mark narrates little by little as the people question: "Who then is this whom even wind and sea obey?" (4:41) "What is this [new doctrine]?" (1:27), "Why does this man speak that way? [...] Who but God alone can forgive sins" (2:7). The answer is not found on one page or in one miracle, but in the entire Gospel.

Mark weaves eighteen of Jesus' miracles into his Gospel. As he heals the sick, he also forgives sins and on four occasions he delivers possessed people. Thus we see how Jesus is able to perform miracles and prodigies, which Mark presents as signs of God's salvation.

In this Gospel, Jesus is always with his disciples, with whom he forms a community (2:23), whom he defends from attacks by the scribes and Pharisees (2:25), even when they do not understand (8:14–21) or when they sleep in Gethsemane (14:37). Peter denies him (14:66), the disciples abandon him (14:50), and they do not believe after the resurrection (16:11–14). Since the Jews expected a powerful and victorious warrior messiah to deliver them from Roman oppression, Jesus called himself the "Son of Man," a more humble title, which Mark mentions fourteen times in his Gospel. The supreme moment in Mark's Gospel is the cross. For Mark, Jesus is the suffering Messiah.

For Mark, Jesus is the Christ, the Messiah, the Son of God (1:1). He begins his Gospel by saying that Jesus is the Christ, which is the Greek word for Messiah, the Son of God (1:1). It is through the Gospel of Mark's sixteen chapters that this statement takes shape. Thus we see how the first part of the claim—Jesus is the Christ—comes from the lips of Peter, who confesses his faith at Caesarea Philippi when he says: "You are the Messiah" (8:29). And the second statement, Jesus is the Son of God, comes from the lips of the Roman captain who saw how Jesus died during the crucifixion: "Truly this man was the Son of God" (15:39).

The Gospel of Mark was the first of the four Gospels to be written, and it had a significant impact on the Church and later writers. In this book one will read how Jesus prepared for his public ministry and how he revealed the mystery of the kingdom of God in his words and by his life.

LOVE in Action

• *In his Gospel, Mark shows us how Jesus is always with his disciples. Does knowing that Jesus is always close to us bring you peace? Share with the group.*

Luke: A Universal Gospel

At the beginning of his Gospel, Luke addresses his friend Theophilus, saying that some people have written about the events that have occurred, and that he also, having carefully researched the matter, considered it fitting to write this story, which is absolutely credible since there have been many reliable witnesses who knew Jesus personally, heard his teachings, and saw his miracles, his death and resurrection, and his ascension into heaven. (1:1–4).

Luke addressed his Gospel to the Gentile Christians, that is, to those who were not Jewish and were unaccustomed to Jewish beliefs and practices. He wrote for Christians living in a society dominated by the Greek culture and language. Precisely for this reason, his Gospel is known as the universal Gospel and it is considered easier to read and understand.

There are more women in the Gospel of Luke than in the other Gospels.

He thought it was important to help these foreign societies see the importance of prayer and the power of intercession. He constantly shows Jesus at prayer: before choosing the twelve (6:12), at the time of the multiplication of the loaves and fish (9:16), during the transfiguration (9:28–29) and at the Last Supper (22:17–19). He intercedes for his friend Peter (22:32). He tells us two parables about the power of prayer: the importunate friend (11:5–13) and the unjust judge (18:1–8).

Since he is writing his Gospel for non-Jews, Luke emphasizes the positive actions of foreigners such as the Samaritan leper who returned to thank Jesus for his healing (17:11–19) and the parable of the Good Samaritan (10:29–37). Christ commended them not only for their gratitude and love, but also for their faith (7:9).

Luke makes it clear that Jesus came to save all men (24:47). Therefore, he presents Jesus as the friend of sinners and the marginalized, as he who came "to seek and to save what was lost" (19:10). He tells the parable of the lost sheep (15:1–10), the widow's coins (21:1–4), and the prodigal son (15:11–32). He eats in the home of Zacchaeus (19:1-10) and brings the good news to the poor (7:22). Only Luke tells the parable of the rich man and Lazarus (16:19–31).

There are more women in the Gospel of Luke than in the other Gospels. We read about Elizabeth (1), the prophetess Anna (2:36–38), the widow of Nain (7:11–17), the woman who anointed Jesus' feet (7:36–50), Mary Magdalene (8:2), the women who traveled with Jesus and the apostles and catered to their needs (8:1–3), Martha and Mary (10:38–42), the poor widow's contribution (21:1–4), and the women who wept at the sight of Jesus carrying the cross (23:27–28).

We cannot finish talking about Luke without mentioning the role that the Holy Spirit plays in his Gospel. The Holy Spirit is present from the Incarnation (1), in the presentation of Jesus in the Temple (2:22–27), and in all of Jesus' activities (4:1, 10:21). Luke highlights the Holy Spirit's availability for all who seek him: "How much more will the Father in heaven give the holy Spirit to those who ask him" (11:13).

Luke shows us that salvation is for everyone, but especially for the poor, the sinners, the sick, and foreigners. His Gospel shows us the meaning of compassion and mercy for the oppressed.

LOVE in Action

• *Luke speaks constantly about prayer and its importance. How is your prayer life? Do you pray before making an important decision?*

John: A Deep and Spiritual Gospel

John writes his Gospel seeking to answer the question: Who is Jesus of Nazareth? He begins by presenting Jesus as the Word who was with God and was God (1:1). By the manner in which it is written along with the focus that John has, this Gospel is very different from the others. It is much more profound, spiritual, and contemplative, so much so that Saint Augustine compares John to an eagle that is capable of flying at high altitudes, indicating that his focus is higher and more sublime than the other three evangelists.

John's Gospel was written several years after the rest of the Gospels, circa 90. This gave John a valuable space of time to reflect more deeply on what Jesus did and said. Thus, he could speak of Jesus in a more spiritual way. In chapter 20, he tells us this Gospel's main purpose: "That you may believe that Jesus is the Messiah, the Son of God" (John 20:31) and that by believing, we may have life in him.

John writes for communities living in a world that was dominated by Greco-Roman values. Therefore, he calls on people's capacity for reflection to come to recognize that Jesus really is who he says he is: "I am the resurrection and the life" (11:25), "I am the good shepherd" (10:11), "I am the light of the world" (8:12), "I am the way and the truth and the life. No one comes to the Father except through me" (14:6).

He seeks to show that Jesus is not just a teacher or a prophet or someone who performs miracles, but he is the Messiah, the Son of God (20:31). For that, he chooses seven miracles, which he presents as "signs" of the power and presence of God among his people. These miracles include: turning water into wine at the wedding at Cana (2:10–12); healing the daughter of the king's servant even when he was far away (4:46–54); healing a man who had been a paralytic for thirty-eight years (5:1–15); multiplying five loaves and two fish that fed the five thousand men who followed him (6:1–15); walking on water to get to the boat where his disciples were and it landing at the place they were heading (6:16–21); healing a man born blind (9:1–12); and raising Lazarus after he had been dead for three days (11:1–44).

All these "signs" let us see that Jesus has authority over creation. They show that Jesus is the master of nature, disease, and death, that he has the power to create, restore, and fix what is broken, lost, or destroyed. These "signs" allow us to see that his power and his kingdom are much greater than all earthly powers. They evince how Jesus, the Son of God, is not only all-powerful, but also merciful and full of love, and that he came into the world out of love so that we could come to God.

In this Gospel, we can learn more about Jesus, for he defines himself seven times, saying that he is the bread of life (6:35), the light of the world (8:12), the gate (10:7), the good shepherd (10:11), the resurrection and the life (11:25), the way, the truth, and the life (14:6) and the true vine (15:1).

The highlight of this Gospel is found in what we know as "the hour of glory."

This is the Gospel of the great dialogues and speeches. Jesus dialogues with Nicodemus (3:1–21) and with the Samaritan woman (4); he speaks with the disciples, particularly Peter and Thomas. And he gives several speeches: the Bread of Life (6:22–59), the Good Shepherd (10:1–21) and the Last Supper discourse (13—17).

He speaks of the sacraments: baptism (3), confirmation (7:39), Eucharist (6), reconciliation (20:22–23), and holy orders (20:21–23). He sanctifies a marriage in Cana by his presence (2:1–11).

The highlight of this Gospel is found in what we know as "the hour of glory": "The hour has come for the Son of Man to be glorified. Amen, amen, I say to you, unless a grain of wheat falls to the ground and dies, it remains just a grain of wheat; but if it dies, it produces much fruit. Whoever loves his life loses it, and whoever hates his life in this world will preserve it for eternal life" (12:23–25). This "hour of glory" is the crucifixion of Jesus; it is the moment when Jesus freely gives his life to the Father out of love for humanity. For John, Jesus reigns from the cross. Jesus himself says that when he is lifted up from the earth, he will draw all people to himself (see 12:32).

Answering the question posed at the beginning about who is Jesus of Nazareth, John gives us the answer by telling us that Jesus is the Word made flesh, the one who existed before creation (1:1), since God so loved the world that "he gave his only Son, so that everyone who believes in him might not perish but might have eternal life" (3:16), to inspire in us a deeper understanding of the love God has for us.

LOVE in Action

- *Jesus says that he is the "bread of life." How can you prepare our souls before receiving Jesus in the Eucharist?*

Acts of the Apostles

Luke's writings are divided into two volumes. The first part of his writings is his Gospel, which presents all that Jesus began to do and teach (1:1). The second part of his work is the Book of the Acts of the Apostles, which tells us that before he ascended into heaven, Jesus said to his followers, "You will receive power when the holy Spirit comes upon you, and you will be my witnesses in Jerusalem, throughout Judea and Samaria, and to the ends of the earth" (1:8).

Acts was written between the years 80 and 90. It tells us how this new era, the time of the Church, began from Jerusalem. It is a time when Jesus' teachings, his words, and his salvation are carried to the ends of the earth, which in those days were the Christian communities of Asia Minor, Macedonia, Greece, and Rome.

Acts begins with the story of the ascension of Jesus into heaven, the election of Matthias as a replacement for Judas, and the coming of the Holy Spirit upon the apostles at Pentecost. It continues by sharing the life experiences of the first Christian community with its many joys and vicissitudes. But the Holy Spirit is the central figure in Acts. The Spirit is conferred upon the apostles at Pentecost (2:1–13) and is the quiet power that leads them in their missionary work and the force that guides the Church in its courageous action.

Much of these Scriptures are focused on Peter's actions and Paul's conversion story along with his missionary journeys. In fact, the two main human characters are Peter and Paul. Peter is the one who draws together the Christians of Palestine into following Jesus the Christ, and Paul is the apostle to the Gentiles, that is, to those who were not Jews.

Furthermore, the Acts of the Apostles tell us also how Paul, who was a great persecutor of the Church, became a great apostle after his conversion. He embarks on three missionary trips to announce the Gospel and establish the faith in Asia Minor and Greece. When he is arrested by the Roman authorities, he is taken to Rome, where he continues to proclaim the Gospel until his death, which is not narrated. The book ends when the Gospel, meaning "the good news," reaches Rome, the end of the earth (1:8).

The Acts of the Apostles tell us how the first Christian community sought to convey what they had received, bearing witness to what they had seen, and acting as a representative for the one who had sent them.

> *"You will receive power when the holy Spirit comes upon you, and you will be my witnesses in Jerusalem, throughout Judea and Samaria, and to the ends of the earth."*

LOVE in Action

- *Paul had his conversion on the road to Damascus. Have you had a strong conversion moment in your life, or has your conversion taken place gradually as you draw closer to Jesus little by little?*

- *Do you connect the mission of the apostles and disciples with your own? The mission of the early Christians has now been passed on to twenty-first-century Christians. How do you witness Jesus' message to others?*

Concluding Prayer: Lord Jesus, you are the fulfillment of all our hopes and desires. Fill us with the joy of the Gospel and inflame our hearts with love for all our brothers and sisters, humankind. Amen.

SUGGESTED RESOURCES:

Alfaro, Juan. *Getting to Know Jesus* (Liguori Publications, 2008).

Liguori Catholic Bible Study (http://www.liguori.org/store/liguori-catholic-bible-study.html).

Lukefahr, Oscar CM. *A Catholic Guide to the Bible* (Liguori Publications, 1998).

Septién, Pía. *Women of the New Testament: Their Lives, Our Hope* (Liguori Publications, 2012).

Septién, Pía. *Women of the Old Testament: Their Lives, Our Hope* (Liguori Publications, 2012).

CINEMA CONNECTION

Some biblical resources:

The Ten Commandments (1956), starring Charlton Heston, Yul Brynner, and Anne Baxter. Cecil B. DeMille's cinema masterpiece tells the Exodus story in great detail.

The Prince of Egypt (1998), with voices by Val Kilmer, Ralph Fiennes, Michelle Pfeiffer, Sandra Bullock, Jeff Goldblum, Danny Glover, Steve Martin, Martin Short. An animated version of the Exodus event, in which Moses calls on Pharaoh to let his people go.

The Bible (2013 TV miniseries). In five parts, this miniseries highlights some of the great events of salvation history.

VeggieTales (1993–2013). Set to music, these tales told by animated vegetable characters highlight stories from the Bible and other stories in order to teach children lessons about faith and life.

The Nativity Story (2006), starring Keisha Castle-Hughes, Oscar Isaac, Hiam Abbass. The story of the nativity of Jesus and the events leading up to it.

Jesus of Nazareth (1977 TV miniseries) with Robert Powell starring as Jesus. The Life of Christ is told using Gospel accounts.

ABOUT THE AUTHOR

Pía Septién is a biblical instructor at the University of Dallas School of Ministry, holds a master's degree in theological studies, and has a certificate in pastoral administration from the University of Dallas. Her bachelor's degree is in business administration from Anahuac University in Mexico City, where she was born and raised. Septién is the mother of five and lives with her husband and children in Greater Dallas.

Notes

The Holy Trinity: Mystery of Love

....
By Fr. Antonio Rivero, LC, PhD

Preparation

Have ready a Bible, a candle, matches, and a cross or Christian icon. Set these up on a small table in front of the room where the group will meet, or in the center if you are using a circle format.

Optional

Prepare some simple refreshments for the group to share either before or after the session.

Have music playing quietly in the background on a CD or iPod as participants arrive and settle in.

Opening *TEN MINUTES*

When everyone is seated, light the candle. Begin with the suggested opening song or use one of your choosing. Or you can go directly to the opening prayer found in the session and have everyone read it aloud together.

Scripture Reading

Matthew 3:13–17

Ask a member of the group to read, or you can read it aloud to the group. Once the passage is read, direct the group members to silently reflect for a minute or two on what they have just heard. This also serves as a centering and quieting exercise for participants.

Supporting catechism quotes for Session Five

"Many religions invoke God as 'Father.' The deity is often considered the 'father of gods and men.' In Israel, God is called Father inasmuch as he is Creator of the world" (CCC 238); see Deuteronomy 32:6; Malachi 2:10.

"Jesus revealed that God is Father in an unheard-of-sense: he is Father not only in being Creator; he is eternally Father in relation to his only Son, who is eternally Son only in relation to his Father: 'No one knows the Son except the Father, and no one knows the Father except the Son and anyone to whom the Son chooses to reveal him'" (CCC 240); see Matthew 11—27.

"The Trinity is One. We do not confess three Gods, but one God in three persons: 'the consubstantial Trinity' (Council of Constantinople II, 553: DS 421). The divine persons do not share the one divinity among themselves but each of them is God whole and entire: The Father is that which the Son is, the Son that which the Father is, the Father and the Son that which the Holy Spirit is, i.e. by nature one God" (CCC 253); Council of Toledo XI (675): DS 530:26.

The Holy Trinity: Mystery of Love

ALLOW FIFTEEN MINUTES FOR EACH SECTION.

Take a few minutes for the group to read through the section, then move to the **LOVE in Action** questions. Allow each person a minute or two to contribute, and give each group member the opportunity to speak.

Additional questions for reflection and discussion

- *Why do we say that the mystery of the Holy Trinity is not contradictory? How do we know that God is one and three?*

- *What are the differences between a soul in the state of grace and a soul that is not?*

- *Why do we say that God is a Father? Why do we say that God is a Son? Why do we say that God is the Holy Spirit?*

Closing Rite

FIVE MINUTES

Invite participants to take part in a few moments of silence, then ask the participants for spontaneous prayer. When finished you can offer this brief blessing to the group:

Oh God! Bless and watch over us while we set out to share your love and the Good News of Jesus Christ with all those we encounter in our daily lives.

Concluding Prayer: I thank you, Lord, with all my heart; in the presence of the angels to you I sing. I bow low toward your holy temple; I praise your name for your mercy and faithfulness. For you have exalted over all your name and your promise. On the day I cried out, you answered; you strengthened my spirit. All the kings of earth will praise you, LORD, when they hear the words of your mouth. They will sing of the ways of the LORD: "How great is the glory of the LORD!" The LORD is on high, but cares for the lowly and knows the proud from afar (Psalm 138).

SESSION

5

The Holy Trinity: Mystery of Love

By Fr. Antonio Rivero, LC, PhD

WHO is the Holy Trinity?

WHAT does Scripture say about the Blessed Trinity?

WHERE do we see the Holy Trinity's love in our lives?

WHEN can we connect with the Blessed Trinity?

WHY are we called to live a life in union with the Trinity?

Opening Song: "Praise God, From Whom All Blessings Flow," by Thomas Ken, or a hymn of your choice

Opening Prayer: Eternal and Blessed Trinity, we praise you and long to see your beauty. During this session, guide us in your goodness, that we might long for you and you alone. Open our hearts to understand, our ears to hear, and our eyes to see your glory in all of creation, particularly in the communities that we exist within: our families, workplaces, service organizations, businesses, and friendships. We thank you for your eternal love. Help us to know you more. Amen.

Reading: Matthew 3:13–17 (baptism of Jesus)

Spend a moment in quiet reflection.

Who Is the Holy Trinity?

The *Catechism of the Catholic Church* tells us that the mystery of the Holy Trinity is the central mystery of faith and Christian life. It is the mystery of God's self and the source of all the other mysteries of faith and the light that enlightens them. The whole history of salvation is simply the story of the way and means by which the one true God—Father, Son, and Holy Spirit—reveals self, and reconciles himself to humanity once we choose to turn away from sin, joining us eternally to the Blessed Trinity. This mystery is so luminous that it dazzles us, and we cannot look at it head on, just as we cannot look directly at the sun.

The mystery of the Holy Trinity can be summarized as follows: in God there are three divine persons: Father, Son, and Holy Spirit. They are the one true God—not three gods, but one. Christ revealed this great mystery during his earthly life to show us God's infinite and gratuitous love for humanity.

> *The Trinity: a mystery God has revealed in Christ.*

The Scriptures

The Trinity is a mystery that God has revealed in Christ. On our own, we would never even have remotely glimpsed it. As a result, humanity is unable to reach and grasp this mystery with the sheer force of reason and intelligence. We need faith, the gift bestowed on us by God on the day of our baptism as a seed we should make grow day by day. By this faith in God, we believe and trust in what God has told us, for God does not deceive us.

In the Old Testament there are several references to this mystery, but God did not teach it in a clear way, perhaps because the Jews, prone to idolatry, would have taken the three divine persons as three gods. Once more I want to emphasize that the Trinity is one God in three persons. Some of the references found in the Old Testament are: The Spirit of God hovered over the waters (Genesis 1:2), let us make man to our image and likeness (Genesis 1:26), the Lord breathed the breath of life into his nostrils (Genesis 2:7), Joshua was full of the spirit of wisdom (Deuteronomy 34:9), the spirit of the Lord came upon Gideon (Judges 6:34), the spirit of God came into the messengers of Saul (1 Samuel 19:20), "the spirit lifted me up and took me away" (Ezekiel 3:14), and "I will pour out my spirit upon all flesh" (Joel 3:1).

In the New Testament there are two very important texts pointing to the three divine persons. The first is Jesus' baptism: "After Jesus was baptized, he came up from the water and behold, the heavens were opened [for him], and he saw the Spirit of God descending like a dove [and] coming upon him. And a voice came from the heavens, saying, 'This is my beloved Son, with whom I am well pleased'" (Matthew 3:16–17). The second is indicated when Christ sent the disciples out to the world to preach conversion: "Go, therefore, and make disciples of all nations, baptizing them in the name of the Father, and of the Son, and of the holy Spirit" (Matthew 28:19). John tells us that the Spirit will lead us into all truth (John 16:13–14), and to "receive the holy Spirit…" (John 20:22). Paul's letters also include references to the person of the Holy Spirit: "And we speak about them not with words taught by human wisdom, but with words taught by the Spirit" (1 Corinthians 2:13); our body is the temple of the Holy Spirit (1 Corinthians 3:16–17); Paul speaks of gifts of the Holy Spirit (1 Corinthians 12:1–11) and of fruits of the Spirit (Galatians 5:22–23). Paul also moves us with that phrase from Ephesians 4:30: "Do not grieve the holy Spirit" or "do not quench the Spirit" (1 Thessalonians 5:19).

Though this mystery is incomprehensible, it is not contradictory. It is incomprehensible because of the excess of light and the depth of its wealth. It would be contradictory if we were saying that there is one person and three persons in God, or one nature and three natures. But this is not the case, as we profess that the Trinity is one God in three persons. We firmly believe this mystery because God has revealed it to us.

How Can We Know the Mystery of the Trinity?

We know with certainty that God exists by the light of natural reason which grasps his existence through the reality of created things. But only through faith in revelation can we know what God is like. Let me explain the unfathomable mystery of the Holy Trinity according to the *Catechism of the Catholic Church* (238–260).

Speaking of the Holy Trinity means talking about the most beautiful and precious mystery that Christians live. To know, believe, and experience that God is a Father who loves us with affection and adopts us as his children in baptism should fill us with deep joy. Our joy and gratitude continue to deepen with our experience and knowledge of Jesus, the Son of God who became incarnate and saved us with his blood, thus breaking the chains of our sins and opening the gates of heaven. Furthermore, knowing God as the Holy Spirit should fill our heart with comfort, our mind with light, and our will with strength. The Spirit is dwelling as a guest in our soul, having accompanied and graced us from the moment of our baptism. Christians are called to reflect the presence of the Holy Trinity in their body and souls through thought, speech, and action.

It is not easy to understand this mystery with our little intelligence. Many questions assail us: Is there any point in believing in the Trinity? What does believing or not believing in the Trinity mean for us? How do we enter the heart of the Holy Trinity and partake of God's infinite love? Can we confuse ourselves with the threefold personhood of God—how is God one in three? Why do other people believe in polytheism, that is, in many gods? What is our Trinitarian God really like?

By faith we can say the following: in the history of salvation, everything begins with the Trinity present in creation, and everything culminates in the Trinity when saved humankind comes face to face with the divine persons. Human beings can share in the love the Trinity bestows and graces us with at our baptism and through the other sacraments. Herein lies the great dignity of humanity: not only are we a reflection of the Holy Trinity, but God actually invites us to participate in that current of love found in the three divine persons—Father, Son, and Holy Spirit.

Our God is one God, but he is not a solitary God. We must learn how to live with diverse people in harmony, love, and unity, as the three persons of the Trinity have shown us, preserving the unity of hearts in the midst of our diversity. In our families, workplaces, parishes, and social groups, God calls us to mirror Trinitarian love by living together in the spirit of community and refraining from quarrels, fights, jealousy, and selfishness.

Parents ought to imitate the love of God and be faithful representatives of God to their children, for the family is also a community of love established by God. Children should see reflected in the actions of their parents the tenderness of God the Father, the wisdom and mercy of God the Son, and the comfort and encouragement of God the Holy Spirit.

LOVE in Action

- *What image do you have of the Blessed Trinity? Name some ways that might expand your imagination about the Blessed Trinity.*

- *How does Scripture and tradition present the Trinitarian God? What images and superstitions tarnish the true image of God? On the contrary, what images serve to enhance our understanding of the triune God?*

- *What are some ways that you relate to God— Father, Son, and Holy Spirit?*

Trinitarian Doctrine

The Nature of the Triune God

As to the nature of the mystery, the three persons are not distinguished either by their nature or by its perfections, nor by their external works. They are distinguished only by their origin:

Not by their nature, because they have a common nature, the divine nature. Therefore, they are not three Gods, but one God.

Not for their perfections, because these are identified with the divine nature. None of the three persons are wiser or more powerful, but they all have infinite wisdom and power. Not one is older than the others, but all are equally eternal.

Nor are they distinguished by their external works, because all three have the same omnipotence, and what one does in relation to us or in the world, the other two do as well.

They are distinguished by their origin because the Father does not come from any other person; the Son is begotten of the Father; and the Holy Spirit proceeds from the love of the Father and the Son. Saint Augustine explained it by saying that the Father begets the Son by knowledge and the Spirit appears as a result of the spiritual love of both.

- The Father is called "Father" because he engendered the second person by way of understanding, that is, by knowing himself, he forms an image of himself that is distinct but perfect like him.
- The Son is called "Son" because he is begotten by the Father. He is also called "Word," that is, the Word of God, for just as a word is the result of human understanding, so the Word is the result of the Father's understanding.
- The third person is called "Spirit," that is, one who expresses the aspiration or impulse of love because this love proceeds from the Father and the Son. The word "Holy" is added to the Spirit's name because holiness is attributed to the same Spirit in a special way.

God in Relationship

As for the activity of the divine persons: God's activity can be internal (*ab intra*) if it refers to the divine persons among themselves, and external (*ad extra*), if it relates to the creatures.

The internal is proper to each of the three divine persons. Fatherhood is attributed to the name of God the Father; filiation to God the Son; and spiration to God the Holy Spirit. Fatherhood is the relationship of the Father to the Son: a relationship of love and tenderness. Filiation is the relationship of the Son to the Father, a relationship of love and filial obedience. Spiration is the relationship of the Father and of the Son to the Spirit: a relationship of mutual love, affection, and giving.

The external is common to the three divine persons, and so whatever one of them does to creatures or the world, so do the other two. But there are certain works that are proper to each one, although not exclusive to them. Such works are especially attributed to each of the divine persons because they have some relation to their origin. Thus Scripture teaches:

- Omnipotence and works of omnipotence, such as the creation and preservation of the world and creatures are often attributed to the Father. As the Father is the beginning of the other divine persons, in a special way he is the origin of all beings.
- Wisdom and works of wisdom, such as redemption and the final judgment, are usually attributed to the Son. Wisdom because it proceeds by way of understanding, and wisdom is the result of understanding.
- Love and works of love, such as the sanctification of souls, are often attributed to the craftsmanship of the Holy Spirit in each of us.

Conflict About Doctrine

It was not always easy to live this dogma of the Trinity, that is, this truth of faith we must believe because God has revealed it to us. There were heresies (doctrinal errors) that denied some aspect or another of this mystery. Historically speaking, the most famous heresies pertaining to the Holy Trinity include the following.

Some, wanting to better secure the oneness of God, denied the trinity of persons, claiming that the three divine persons were only three different ways to conceive of God, rather than three distinct persons. The heretic named Sabellius believed that there was only one person, the Father, and that the other two were only forms of God the Father. His heresy was called *modalism*, because he believed that one person was greater than the other two, when Christians profess that all three possess equal divinity.

Others, wanting to better secure the difference of persons, came to deny their equal nature. For example, Arius, who denied the divinity of Christ, said the Son was of a different nature than the Father. Macedonius, in turn, denied the divinity of the Holy Spirit.

LOVE in Action

- *How do you bring the mystery of the Holy Trinity into your life?*

- *Is it difficult for you to grasp the doctrine of the Holy Spirit? In what way?*

Trinitarian Love Manifested in Our Lives

The Holy Trinity is dwelling in our souls through the grace of our baptism, enriching them with theological virtues and the gifts of the Holy Spirit. Thus, we can be holy and act supernaturally in our lives, loving and worshiping God, and loving others as God loves. The union of our soul with God's grace is so real that it can be called physical-moral. This union with God is not seen physically, but by works. People who possess God through grace feel more encouraged every day to put the virtues and gifts into action.

The Indwelling of the Trinity

Since Christian life is a participation in God's very life, it is clear that only God can give divine life to us. By placing God's very self in our souls, we are able to worship, enjoy, and docilely let ourselves be ruled by our triune God, so as to imitate Christ's virtues and example.

We know God inhabits creatures naturally in three ways: **by God's power**, because nothing escapes his domain; **by God's presence**, because he is everywhere; and **by God's essence**, because he created all that exists.

God's presence in us by grace is of a more sublime and intimate order. It is not only the presence of the Creator or conserver who maintains that which was created into being. The holy and adorable Trinity dwell in us, just as faith reveals it to us. The Father comes to us and continues to engender his Word in us; together with the Father, we receive the Son, fully equal to the Father and his living image, who eternally and infinitely loves his Father, and who is also infinitely loved by him. From this mutual love flows the Holy Spirit, a person equal to the Father and the Son, the mutual bond that links the two, and yet, distinct from both of them. How many wonders take place in a soul in grace!

The presence of God is characterized by the intimacy of the Blessed Trinity—God is not only in us, but gives freely of self so that we might enjoy him. We receive God as father, mother, friend, coworker, and sanctifier; the very principle of our interior life.

God as Father

This divine life in us, as adopted children of God, is a participation, a likeness, an assimilation, that does not make us gods, but "godlike." It is a reality, a new life, not equal to but similar to that of God. According to Scripture, it is a new generation or regeneration: Unless one is born of water and Spirit. He saved us through the bath of rebirth and renewal by the holy Spirit. Blessed be the God and Father of our Lord Jesus Christ, who in his great mercy gave us a new birth to a living hope through the resurrection of Jesus Christ from the dead. He willed to give us birth by the word of truth that we may be a kind of firstfruits of his creatures (see John 3:5, Titus 3:5, 1 Peter 1:3; James 1:18).

For this reason, we are heirs with full rights to the kingdom of heaven, heirs of the one who is our elder brother (see Romans 8:17, 8:29). John tells us: "See what love the Father has bestowed on us that we may be called the children of God. Yet so we are. The reason the world does not know us is that it did not know him" (1 John 3:1).

God will have the tenderness of a father for us. He compares himself to a mother who cannot ever forget her child (see Isaiah 49:15). The Lord demonstrates this by delivering up and sacrificing his only Son, so that none of us would lose him (see John 3:16).

God as Friend

Friendship adds some type of equality, a certain intimacy and reciprocity, which carries with it a very sweet communication. God really reveals his secrets to us; he speaks through the Church and inwardly by the Holy Spirit. So at the Last Supper Jesus tells us that we are his friends, for he keeps no secrets from us (see John 15:15).

A most loving familiarity anoints the relations between God and the soul; it is the familiarity of friends who get together for dinner: "Behold, I stand at the door and knock. If anyone hears my voice and opens the door, [then] I will enter his house and dine with him, and he with me" (Revelation 3:20). It is a wonderful intimacy that we would never have dared to ask for had it not been offered to us by our divine friend!

God as Partner

The Lord knows that by our own strength we cannot take care of our supernatural life, which is why he remedies our powerlessness, strengthens our will, enlightens our minds, gives us the necessary encouragement, and instills enthusiasm and the certainty of victory against our enemies. God, who began a good work in our sanctification, will bring it to fruition (see Philippians 1:6). Therefore, we are never alone, even when we are devoid of all comfort and seem to have been abandoned. The grace of God will always be with us as long as we desire it. Relying on such a powerful partner, we will be invincible, because we can do all things in him who strengthens us (see Philippians 4:13).

God as Sanctifier

By coming to dwell in our soul, God transforms it into a holy temple enriched with all the virtues (see 1 Corinthians 3:17). The God who comes to us by grace is the living God, the Holy Trinity, the infinite source of divine life, who seeks nothing but to make us partakers of his holiness. This indwelling in the soul is attributed to the Holy Spirit by appropriation as a work of love, but since it is also a work "*ad extra*," it is common to the three divine persons. Thus Saint Paul calls us both temples of God and temples of the Holy Spirit (see 1 Corinthians 3:16).

Therefore, our soul is the temple of the living God, a sacred citadel reserved for God, a throne of mercy where God is pleased to pour out his heavenly favors adorned with all the virtues. Working and living in us, the Holy Trinity sanctifies us.

Duties Toward the Holy Trinity

- Give the triune God our homage of adoration and love. We have no other god but the Trinity. We must destroy our small or large idols. Every time we kneel in prayer, we lessen these idols by coming to know more intimately God's life and love.

- Thank God for the immense benefits of creation, Incarnation, redemption, and sanctification. We are made to participate in divine love. The many graces we have received from the Holy Trinity will make us eternally grateful.

- Entrust ourselves to the three divine persons, the source of light, hope, and love for Christians in every moment of our day, from the time we awake until we fall asleep at night, through the prayers: "Glory be to the Father and to the Son and to the Holy Spirit" and also "In the name of the Father and of the Son and of the Holy Spirit. Amen." Entrust oneself to the Father so that he will grant us mighty paternal power and love; to the Son, that his holy blood may cleanse our sins and that his body may nourish our hunger for happiness; to the Holy Spirit so that he may deign to enlighten us on the way of life and comfort us in the times of grief and sorrow that we experience in our journey toward heaven.

LOVE in Action

- *Name some ways that the Spirit of God has moved you.*

- *What are some ways that your generosity mirrors that of the Blessed Trinity? Are you able to freely give yourself to those who are hurtful/sinful?*

Concluding Prayer: I thank you, Lord, with all my heart; in the presence of the angels to you I sing. I bow low toward your holy temple; I praise your name for your mercy and faithfulness. For you have exalted over all your name and your promise. On the day I cried out, you answered; you strengthened my spirit. All the kings of earth will praise you, LORD, when they hear the words of your mouth. They will sing of the ways of the LORD: "How great is the glory of the LORD!" The LORD is on high, but cares for the lowly and knows the proud from afar (Psalm 138).

SUGGESTED RESOURCES

Augustine of Hippo. *The Trinity* (2003, New City Press).

Greshem, John L. PhD. *Holy Spirit 101: Present Among Us* (Liguori Publications, 2011).

Greshem, John L. PhD. *Jesus 101: God and Man* (Liguori Publications, 2011).

Papandrea, James L. MDiv, PhD. *Trinity 101: Father, Son, and Holy Spirit* (Liguori Publications, 2012).

CINEMA CONNECTION

The Chronicles of Narnia: The Lion, the Witch, and the Wardrobe (2005), starring Georgie Henley, Skandar Keynes, William Moseley, Anna Popplewell. Four children enter a wardrobe that lands them in another world known as Narnia. Based on a book by C.S. Lewis.

Finding Nemo (2003), with voices by Albert Brooks, Ellen DeGeneres, Alexander Gould. A father clown-fish witnesses the capture of his son Nemo and sets out on a long journey to find him.

Changing Lanes (2002), starring Ben Affleck, Samuel L. Jackson, Kim Staunton. A story that begins with rage and a feud eventually leads the two main characters to a new outlook on life.

ABOUT THE AUTHOR

Fr. Antonio Rivero, LC, PhD, is a Spanish priest who teaches theology and oratory at the Maria Mater Ecclesiae International Seminary in Sao Paulo, Brazil. He has taught seminarians in Mexico and Spain, and he has been a pastor in Buenos Aires. Rivero has written books and has recorded more than 200 educational compact discs. He has lectured in the United States on several topics, including Catholic faith formation. He holds a doctorate in spiritual theology from the Pontifical Athenaeum Regina Apostolorum in Rome. Also in Rome, he earned bachelor's degrees in philosophy from Gregorian University and in theology from St. Thomas Aquinas University.

SESSION 6

The Eucharist Makes the Church

By Frederick Hermann

Preparation

Have ready a Bible, a candle, matches, and a cross or Christian icon. Set these up on a small table in front of the room where the group will meet, or in the center if you are using a circle format.

Optional

Prepare some simple refreshments for the group to share either before or after the session.

Have music playing quietly in the background on a CD or iPod as participants arrive and settle in.

Opening *TEN MINUTES*

When everyone is seated, light the candle. Begin with the suggested opening song or use one of your choosing. Or you can go directly to the opening prayer found in the session and have everyone read it aloud together.

Scripture Reading

Matthew 26:26–28

Ask a member of the group to read, or you can read it aloud to the group. Once the passage is read, direct the group members to silently reflect for a minute or two on what they have just heard. This also serves as a centering and quieting exercise for participants.

Supporting catechism quotes for Session Six

"The liturgy [Mass] is the work of the whole Christ, head and body. Our high priest celebrates it unceasingly in the heavenly liturgy, with the holy Mother of God, the apostles, all the saints, and the multitude of those who have already entered the kingdom" (CCC 1187).

"At the Last Supper, on the night he was betrayed, our Savior instituted the Eucharistic sacrifice of his Body and Blood. This he did in order to perpetuate the sacrifice of the cross throughout the ages until he should come again, and so to entrust to his beloved Spouse, the Church, a memorial of his death and resurrection: a sacrament of love, a sign of unity, a bond of charity, a Paschal banquet 'in which Christ is consumed, the mind is filled with grace, and a pledge of future glory is given to us" (CCC 1323).

"The Eucharist is 'the source and summit of the Christian life.' 'The other sacraments, and indeed all ecclesiastical ministries and works of the apostolate, are bound up with the Eucharist and are oriented toward it. For in the blessed Eucharist is contained the whole spiritual good of the Church, namely Christ himself, our Pasch'" (CCC 1324); LG 11; PO 5.

The Eucharist Makes the Church

ALLOW FIFTEEN MINUTES FOR EACH SECTION.

Take a few minutes for the group to read through the section, then move to the **LOVE in Action** questions. Allow each person a minute or two to contribute, and give each group member the opportunity to speak.

Additional questions for reflection and discussion

- *Why do we believe that the Eucharist is the "source and summit" of our faith? And why do we say the Eucharist "makes" the Church?*

- *What is the Mass and why do we celebrate it?*

- *How can you explain the fact that the Mass has been celebrated for more than 2,000 years? While we have seen entire civilizations rise and fall, why has the Mass persisted from Jesus' time to the present day?*

- *Compared to the disciples at the Last Supper, do we have a greater understanding of the Eucharist? Explain.*

- *Describe what our Catholic faith would be like if Jesus had never said to the disciples at the Last Supper, "Do this in memory of me."*

Closing Rite
FIVE MINUTES

Invite participants to take part in a few moments of silence, then conclude the lesson with this popular prayer written by Saint Francis of Assisi:

Lord, make me an instrument of your peace.
Where there is hatred, let me sow love;
where there is injury, pardon;
where there is doubt, faith;
where there is despair, hope;
where there is darkness, light;
and where there is sadness, joy.

O Divine Master, grant that I may not so much
*   seek to be consoled as to console;*
to be understood as to understand;
to be loved as to love.
For it is in giving that we receive;
it is in pardoning that we are pardoned;
it is in dying that we are born again to eternal life.
Amen.

When finished you can offer this brief blessing to the group:

The LORD bless you and keep you!

The LORD let his face shine upon you, and be gracious to you!

The LORD look upon you kindly and give you peace! (Numbers 6: 24–26)

Concluding Prayer: *by Thomas Aquinas on the feast of Corpus Christi:* O sacred banquet, in which Christ is received, the memory of His Passion is renewed, the mind is filled with grace, and a pledge of future glory is given to us. Amen.

The Eucharist Makes the Church

By Frederick Hermann

WHO is fully present in the Eucharist?

WHAT is the effect of receiving the Eucharist?

WHERE is the Church made visible?

WHEN did Jesus establish Communion?

WHY is the Eucharist called "the source and summit" of our Catholic faith?

Opening Song: "Holy God, We Praise Thy Name," by Ignaz Franz, or a hymn of your choice

Opening Prayer: *by Saint Thérèse of Lisieux*

May today there be peace within.

May you trust God that you are exactly where you are meant to be.

May you not forget the infinite possibilities that are born of faith.

May you use those gifts that you have received, and pass on the love that has been given to you.

May you be content knowing you are a child of God.

Let this presence settle into your bones, and allow your soul the freedom to sing, dance, praise, and love.

It is there for each and every one of us.

Reading: Matthew 26:26–28 (the Lord's Supper)

Spend a moment in quiet reflection.

What Is the Eucharist?

The Eucharist "makes" the Church, for it is the central mystery to the spiritual life of every Catholic believer, the "source and summit" of our faith (*CCC* 1324). During this session we will explore this great mystery of our faith and how Jesus Christ nourishes us with his flesh and blood and is broken and shared for us in the Eucharist. Why is the Eucharist central to our faith?

As Catholic Christians, we believe Christ is fully present in the Eucharist, and we profess that the consecrated bread and wine change into the Body, Blood, soul, and divinity of our Lord Jesus. Though "Eucharist" is another name for Holy Communion, we also can use the word "Eucharist" to refer to the Mass itself as we gather together as the people of God.

So in order to best understand the mystery of the Eucharist, we must take a look at it in its proper context—the Mass. The five great elements that compose the Mass include the proclaimed Word of God, memorial, sacrifice, thanksgiving, and mission. As we proceed, we will explore further these elements that make up our worship. As we do so, remember that "the mystery of Christ is so unfathomably rich that it cannot be exhausted" (*CCC* 1201).

The Proclaimed Word of God

Somewhere on the planet, every hour of every day, in every time zone, faithful believers like you and me are gathering together just like the early disciples to recall and proclaim anew the words of Jesus, and to re-experience that moment in time which he made timeless. While the Mass is a very personal experience, it is essentially a shared experience, like a family meal, shared by fellow believers all over the world.

> *We can also use the word "Eucharist" to refer to the Mass itself.*

Think about the fact that the Catholic Church is a worldwide body. The same words are spoken in hundreds of different languages. We gratefully remember the sacrifice Jesus made for us and participate in his sacrifice by receiving Holy Communion.

As the Mass begins, we hear the proclamation of the word of God. Four readings from sacred Scripture are proclaimed during the *Liturgy of the Word* every Sunday or feast day, and three on every weekday. On Sundays and feast days, the first reading and responsorial psalm both are taken from the Old Testament, while the second reading and the Gospel are generally from the New Testament. Typically these readings relate to each other and form a distinct theme for the Mass each week. They are then repeated in three-year cycles, so if you attend Mass for three years, you could learn the Bible well.

The entirety of Catholic worship, the Mass, is derived from Scripture. For we believe that Scripture is the word of God. Also, though we do not always think it so, the Word of God is God's own self as the Gospel of John tells us: "In the beginning was the Word, and the Word was with God, and the Word was God" (John 1:1).

On a deeper level, we believe that the Word of God actually became flesh in the person of Jesus; "the Word became flesh" (John 1:14). The Incarnation of our Lord is the eternal Word of God made flesh.

Thus when we hear the word of God and believe it, we not only receive the wisdom of God, we also receive God. Furthermore, God's word has the power to transform us. Why is this difficult for us to believe? Remember that God spoke the universe into existence—think about that the next time you look up at the stars! God's word is powerful beyond our wildest imaginings.

The words we hear, speak, pray, and sing at Mass are powerfully creative, profound, eternal, and therefore capable of changing us instantly. When we obey the word of God, in essence God's will, we are allowing ourselves to be informed by God—conformed and transformed into his likeness.

It is hard to believe that hearing the word of God can transform us, but that is exactly what is happening at every Mass, and every time we hear the word, speak it, or think about it. The prophet Isaiah utters, "so shall my word be that goes forth from my mouth; It shall not return to me empty, but shall do what pleases me, achieving the end for which I sent it" (Isaiah 55:11). As we will see in the next section, the word of God is most powerfully experienced in the person of Jesus in the Eucharist.

LOVE in Action

- *Note the places in the Mass that are based upon Scripture. Where do you hear the word of God in our worship outside of the readings?*

- *What is the relationship between the word and God's self?*

- *How do we encounter God in Scripture?*

- *Share an experience where the word of God has moved you. What was powerful about this experience?*

- *How might reading, hearing, speaking, or praying a verse from Scripture transform us?*

Do This in Remembrance of Me

What do we remember during every eucharistic celebration? Let's go back to where it all began and imagine ourselves sitting around a wooden table with Jesus more than 2,000 years ago.

Jesus broke bread, gave it to his disciples, and said, "Do this in memory of me" (Luke 22:19).

Clearly Jesus wanted his disciples to remember him and his teachings by gathering as a group and sharing a meal together. But Jesus also asked his followers to remember him in a special way by eating his flesh and drinking his blood. What could this mean?

This strange request must have astonished and confused his disciples around the table. In fact, in the bread of life discourse in the Gospel of John, we hear of how this notion troubled the disciples greatly, causing some of them to depart. What did Jesus mean by enacting this memorial of his life? Naturally Jesus wanted his disciples to follow him by imitating the way he lived and by continuing to proclaim his teachings. But he also asked his early followers to share his Body and Blood—a request they must have only dimly understood.

Entering into the life of Jesus by receiving Holy Communion remains a deep mystery—one that can only be understood in the light of faith with the grace of God. However today, with the benefit of centuries of hindsight, we understand more fully that Jesus invites us into mystical communion with him in order to form a single body—the people of God.

At the Eucharist we remember the cross of Jesus—the sacrifice that opens for us a way to God. For Jesus' earthshaking and life-giving sacrifice on the cross has opened heaven for us. Though the world often sees the scandal of the cross as nonsense, this historical moment became Jesus' hour of glory. The Word Made Flesh took on all the sorrows and sins of the world in this eternal sacrifice, taking on our shame in order to make us whole once again. Through his suffering, death, and resurrection into eternal life, Jesus has invited us to join him as we sojourn this life toward eternal life.

It is important to keep in mind that Jesus' command for us to remember his death and resurrection is not just a past event; Christ is present to us in the Eucharist today, accompanying us in this life. At every Mass, we enter into the life of Jesus through word and sacrament, strengthened and encouraged to become leaven for the world. By remembering Jesus we anticipate the future, when Christ will draw all of creation to himself in a final loving embrace, and our praise and thanksgiving will join with the choirs of heaven in eternal song:

> "At the Last Supper, on the night he was betrayed, our Savior instituted the eucharistic sacrifice of his Body and Blood. This he did in order to perpetuate the sacrifice of the cross throughout the ages until he should come again, and so to entrust to his beloved Spouse, the Church, a memorial of his death and resurrection: a sacrament of love, a sign of unity, a bond of charity, a Paschal banquet 'in which Christ is consumed, the mind is filled with grace, and a pledge of future glory is given to us'" (*CCC* 1323).

At Mass we also celebrate and remember those who have gone before us—the saints. We recall the holy Mother of God (Jesus' first disciple), the apostles, the martyrs, and all other saints who have been faithful to the Gospel.

So what is the point in remembering the life, death, and resurrection of Jesus? It is not to direct us backward to a time long ago—though Jesus' story is also our story. And our recollection of his life narrates our stories—our way to God. But why does our Lord tell us to "do this in memory of me?" Jesus offers us his abundant life in the present in order to guide us lovingly to our future life in God—a life that is both divine and eternal.

LOVE in Action

- *If you were a disciple at the Last Supper and Jesus said, "Do this in memory of me," what would you think?*

- *When you remember Jesus at Mass, does the memory of his suffering make you sad? Why or why not?*

- *Does the memory of Jesus' resurrection make you joyful? Share your thoughts on the resurrection event.*

Sacrifice

Now we encounter the most profound mystery of our faith—the sacrifice of the Eucharist. Here before us on the altar we enter into the ultimate sacrifice of Jesus, whose life is poured out for us; Christ's flesh and blood provide divine nourishment for our bodies and souls. Here we taste and see the Creator of the universe and meet the Lord.

The eucharistic celebration is the summit of the Mass, for we are entering into the supreme delight of God's love. For each person, receiving Jesus in Holy Communion is a personal experience, the most intimate encounter we can have in this earthly life with the person of Jesus. When we receive Jesus in the Eucharist, we receive his Body, Blood, soul, and divinity.

Listen carefully to Jesus as he announced his sacrifice to the disciples:

> "Then he took the bread, said the blessing, broke it, and gave it to them, saying, 'This is my body, which will be given for you; do this in memory of me.' And likewise the cup after they had eaten, saying, 'This cup is the new covenant in my blood, which will be shed for you'" (Luke 22:19–20).

At the Last Supper, Jesus gave new meaning to the Jewish celebration of the feast of Passover. By offering himself (instead of a lamb) as the sacrifice, Jesus became the new Passover, also called the New Covenant. Jesus' final sacrifice on the cross atones for all our sins (past, present, and future), and reconciles our broken relationship with God. His self-sacrifice on Calvary has reunited us to God. At every Eucharist this eternal sacrifice is received—for the sacrifice Jesus suffered at Golgotha has been broken and poured out for all.

How is this possible? At ordinary meals, when we eat natural food, we consume and digest what we eat and it becomes a part of us—the energy from the nutrients being absorbed and transformed in our bodies. By contrast, when we consume the Eucharist, the person of Jesus transforms us. He comes to dwell in us and we are made into his image and likeness. As a result, we are transfigured and enabled to share in the blessed life of the Trinity; the Father, the Son, and the Holy Spirit. By taking the place of the sacrificial lamb, Jesus frees us from our sins (and promises to accompany us in this life: "I will be with you always, until the end of time.")

In the Eucharist, we become what we eat. Though Jesus' sacrifice atoned for our sins once for all, Jesus nourishes the body of Christ to become what is being received—we become Christ for the world. Our eucharistic life in Jesus is strengthened by our personal sacrifices. In the Eucharist, we also surrender ourselves to the Father.

Through the Eucharist, the sacrifice that Christ made on the cross is joined to our own sacrifices. Because Christ unites us with himself in Holy Communion, he unites our human suffering with his suffering. As members of his body, our suffering becomes his suffering. When we die to ourselves, in big ways and small, our suffering acquires new meaning because it serves, with Christ on the cross, to redeem the whole world.

When you offer up your daily aches and pains, you are building up the people of God by uniting your pain to the agony in those spiritually starving for the light of Jesus. What a comforting thought! How can you offer up your small pains for those who are in need of Christ's love?

LOVE in Action

- *Jesus sacrificed his life. How do we share in his sacrifice and suffering?*
- *If we offer our bodies as living sacrifices to God, what good does that do?*
- *Is your suffering meaningful? If so, how?*
- *How is suffering redemptive?*

Thanksgiving

The entire celebration of the Eucharist is an act of thanksgiving. We praise God for what his Son Jesus accomplished on the cross by his suffering and his resurrection. In fact, the word "Eucharist" means "thanksgiving." Throughout the Mass, we express our profound gratitude in prayer and praise, word and gesture, song and silence—in gratitude for the gift of the Eucharist that gives us the grace to rejoice in the promise of eternal life.

Eucharist gives us the grace to rejoice in the promise of eternal life.

What are we thankful for specifically? First, we are grateful to God for being who he is: perfect Truth, perfect Love. At every Mass we praise him by saying, "Our Father, who art in heaven, hallowed be thy name." In other words, we praise him for his existence, apart from ourselves. It is good to know the universe is safe!

Second, we appreciate everything God makes in his creation. In Genesis we learn how God created the entire universe and called it "good," then he created man and woman and called them "very good." It was only because of human disobedience that sin entered into the world.

Third, we are specifically thankful during the Mass for the bread and wine, work of human hands. For the Jewish people, these traditional items are served during the Passover meal, for they recall for them the sojourn in the desert when they ate manna provided daily for them by God. God alone sustained them for a time. For us Christians, the bread and wine become the flesh and blood of Jesus poured out for us, in order to like-wise sustain us for eternal life. Jesus is our nourishment for the journey toward God.

Fourth, we are especially grateful for the forgiveness of our sins. We praise God for his mercy and power in choosing to send his only begotten Son to suffer and die as a sacrifice for the forgiveness of our sins, redeeming us along with all of creation.

We are filled with gratefulness as we envision Christ in his role as high priest, sitting next to the Father in heaven, smiling as he draws us all to himself in the Eucharist. So we give our thanks during every eucharistic celebration for what God has done in the past in creation, what he is doing in the present by sanctifying us, and what he will do in the future by redeeming us to live forever with him in heaven.

"The liturgy [Mass] is the work of the whole Christ, head and body. Our high priest celebrates it unceasingly in the heavenly liturgy, with the holy Mother of God, the apostles, all the saints, and the multitude of those who have already entered the kingdom" (*CCC* 1187).

LOVE in Action

- *Thank God for your past blessings—can you name three?*

- *Count your blessings today by making a list of the good things in your life today.*

- *Thank God for blessing other people with abundance. Do you rejoice with those who are joyful?*

- *Praise God for all future blessings that you do not see as yet.*

Mission

The final feature of each eucharistic celebration occurs at the end of every Mass when the priest or deacon exhorts us to go forth and spread the Good News. Once we have received the love of God, we are "sent forth" into the world on an exciting mission to give his love to other people. (In Latin the word for Mass is *missio*, which means "to send.")

These words echo Jesus' command to his disciples when he sent them forth with very specific instructions; "Go into the whole world and proclaim the gospel to every creature" (Mark 16:15). Therefore, we are all missionaries, today and every day, to everyone we meet. Our mission is to proclaim the "Good News" to others in appealing ways that will draw them to Christ, and to be Christ for others!

The Lord is asking that we let our lives reflect the loving image of Jesus to a lonely world. When other people see and come to know us, do they see Jesus? The Lord has called each of us and sends us to be light for the world and salt for the earth. May people hear Jesus' words coming from you; glimpse his smile and feel his touch in yours. In word, action, and deed we become Jesus for others. Our love may be the only experience that others will ever have of the love of God. So love others the way Christ loves you: "We know that we have passed from death to life because we love our brothers" (1 John 3:14). By living and loving others this way, we might lead some (or many) to Christ.

In this mission of love, remember that we do not go forth alone. We go forth with Jesus at our sides. Recall his promise; "I am with you always, until the end of the age" (Matthew 28:20).

Perhaps you may think, "I am useless to God as a missionary because I cannot go out into the world." Nevertheless, you can still go forth supernaturally in prayer. Even if you are confined to your home, a hospital, or prison, you can still pray for others. Everyone needs prayer! Pray for their hopes, dreams, health, and families. With the Holy Spirit as your guide, pray with faith and with constancy. Pray for the Church, for the needs of the world, for the poor, peace on earth, and family life.

LOVE in Action

- *Do you see yourself as a missionary? Why or why not?*

- *Name a concrete way that you might be a light for someone in your life today.*

- *How do you set aside your needs for the needs of others (particularly the poor or spiritually poor)?*

Concluding Prayer: *by Thomas Aquinas on the feast of Corpus Christi:* O sacred banquet, in which Christ is received, the memory of His Passion is renewed, the mind is filled with grace, and a pledge of future glory is given to us. Amen.

SUGGESTED RESOURCES:

Blessed Pope John Paul II. *Apostolic Letter Mane nobiscum Domine* (*On the Year of the Eucharist*, 2004).

Blessed Pope John Paul II. *Letter Dominicae Cenae* (*On the Mystery and Worship of the Eucharist*, 1980).

Blessed Pope John Paul II. *Encyclical Ecclesia de Eucharistia* (*On the Eucharist in Its Relationship to the Church*, 2003).

Caussaude, Jean Pierre de. *Abandonment to Divine Providence.*

Documents of the Second Vatican Council. The Dogmatic Constitution on the Church (*Lumen Gentium*), especially Chapter II, 1964.

Emeritus Pope Benedict XVI. *Deus Caritas Est (God Is Love)*, 5–8, 2005.

Emeritus Pope Benedict XVI. *Apostolic Exhortation Sacramentum Caritatis (On the Eucharist as the Source and Summit of the Church's Life and Mission)*, 2007.

Libreria Editrice Vaticana. *Catechism of the Catholic Church* 1322–1419.

Pope Leo XIII. *Encyclical Mirae Caritatis (On the Holy Eucharist)*, 1902.

Pope Paul VI. *Encyclical Mysterium Fidei (On the Holy Eucharist)*, 1965.

Pope Pius XII. *Encyclical Mediator Dei (On the Sacred Liturgy)*, 1947.

CINEMA CONNECTION

Babette's Feast (1987), in Danish with English subtitles, starring Stéphane Audran, Bodil Kjer, Birgitte Federspiel. This is a beautifully told story of a refugee chef who is befriended by two elderly, suspicious sisters. Babette's generous gift, in the form of a fine dinner for them, and their suspicious group of believers, breaks down barriers and lays the foundation for new beginnings.

Of Gods and Men (2010), in French with English subtitles, starring Lambert Wilson, Michael Lonsdale, Olivier Rabourdin, Philippe Laudenbach, Jacques Herlin, Loïc Pichon, Xavier Maly, Jean-Marie Frin. Set in an impoverished town in Algeria, Trappist monks lead a quiet life but have to decide whether or not to stay in their home when threatened by a terrorist group.

ABOUT THE AUTHOR

Frederick Hermann is the author of *The Joyful Catholic* and *The Spirit Set Me Free*. He is also the author of "Missalette Scripture Reflections" for World Library Publications. He lives in St. Louis with two big dogs who are allowed to sleep on the bed if their paws are dry.

Grace Abounds

By Kathleen Atkinson, OSB

Preparation

Have ready a Bible, a candle, matches, and a cross or Christian icon. Set these up on a small table in front of the room where the group will meet, or in the center if you are using a circle format.

Optional

Prepare some simple refreshments for the group to share either before or after the session.

Have music playing quietly in the background on a CD or iPod as participants arrive and settle in.

Opening *TEN MINUTES*

When everyone is seated, light the candle. Begin with the suggested opening song or use one of your choosing. Or you can go directly to the opening prayer found in the session and have everyone read it aloud together.

Scripture Reading

Proverbs 8:22–31

Ask a member of the group to read, or you can read it aloud to the group. Once the passage is read, direct the group to silently reflect for a minute or two on what they have just heard. This also serves as a centering and quieting exercise for participants.

Supporting catechism quotes for Session Seven

"The practice of goodness is accompanied by spontaneous spiritual joy and moral beauty. Likewise, truth carries with it the joy and splendor of spiritual beauty. Truth is beautiful in itself. Truth in words, the rational expression of the knowledge of created and uncreated reality, is necessary to man, who is endowed with intellect. But truth can also find other complementary forms of human expression, above all when it is a matter of evoking what is beyond words: the depths of the human heart, the exaltations of the soul, the mystery of God" (CCC 2500).

"'The beauty of the images moves me to contemplation, as a meadow delights the eyes and subtly infuses the soul with the glory of God.' Similarly, the contemplation of sacred icons, united with meditation on the Word of God and the singing of liturgical hymns, enters into the harmony of the signs of celebration so that the mystery celebrated is imprinted in the heart's memory and is then expressed in the new life of the faithful" (CCC 1162); Saint John Damascene, De imag. 1, 27: PG 94, 1268A, B.

"'The musical tradition of the universal Church is a treasure of inestimable value, greater even than that of any other art. The main reason for this pre-eminence is that, as a combination of sacred music and words, it forms a necessary or integral part of solemn liturgy'" (CCC 1156); SC 112.

Grace Abounds

ALLOW FIFTEEN MINUTES FOR EACH SECTION.

Take a few minutes for the group to read through the section, then move to the **LOVE in Action** questions. Allow each person a minute or two to contribute, and give each group member the opportunity to speak.

Additional questions for reflection and discussion

- *Where are the places and times in your life that open you to the beauty of God?*

- *How do you nurture these practices?*

- *How does space play a role in your life? —Are you chaotic and overcrowded in the physical space in which you live and work? In your mind and thoughts? In your spiritual self? —How does this keep you from living creatively, making of your life a masterpiece work of art?*

- *There is a familiar campfire song, "Make new friends but keep the old. One is silver, the other is gold." How does this relate to our contemporary experience of music in the Catholic Church?*

Closing Rite

FIVE MINUTES

Invite participants to take part in a few moments of silence, then ask the participants for spontaneous prayer. When finished you can offer this brief blessing to the group:

May God bless us with hearts that sing and minds that dream so that we may give God glory in the masterpiece of our lives.

Concluding Prayer: *Conclude the lesson by praying this version of Psalm 150 antiphonally:*

All   Praise the LORD!
Praise God in his sanctuary; praise him in his mighty firmament!

Side 1   Praise him for his mighty deeds;
Praise him according to his surpassing greatness!

Side 2   Praise him with trumpet sound;
Praise him with lute and harp!

Side 1   Praise him with tambourine and dance;
Praise him with strings and pipe!

Side 2   Praise him with clanging cymbals;
Praise him with loud clashing cymbals!

All   Let everything that breathes praise the LORD!
Praise the LORD!

Grace Abounds

By Kathleen Atkinson, OSB

WHO are some of the great artists in our Catholic tradition?

WHAT relation do literature, art, and music have to our faith?

WHERE can we find examples of Catholic literature?

WHEN were some of the great classical Mass settings composed?

WHY does the Catholic Church value the arts?

Opening Song: "The Call: How Brightly Deep," by Suzanne Toolan, or a hymn of your choice

Opening Prayer: Divine Creator, bless all who use their gifts to bring inspiration and beauty to our lives. Open our eyes that we may see you in color and curve. Open our minds that we may fathom you in word and metaphor. Open our ears that we may hear you in tone and silence. Open our hearts that our time together may bring us closer to you and to one another. Amen.

Reading: Proverbs 8:22–31 (on wisdom)

Spend a moment in quiet reflection.

Introduction

We carry a grace-filled artistic treasure in our Catholic heritage from the earliest of days: The anguish of Dante's *Divine Comedy*. The triumph of Handel's *Hallelujah Chorus*. The incredulity of Michelangelo's ceiling in the Sistine Chapel. This rich Catholic heritage that is ours in literature, art, and music cries out to us of a God who cannot be confined to dogma and logic.

We can become numb to the chaos in which we live, rushing along with pride in our ability to multi-task. Still, God breaks through the clamor and asks us to take notice of tenderness, beauty, and mystery. God asks us to release our clenched minds and allow ourselves to be captivated by the sound, color, shape, and silence with

God asks us to be captivated by the sound, color, shape, and silence with which he has filled all creation.

which God has filled all creation. It is grace. It invites us into a childlike openness to the wonder of living. It connects us to God.

Blessed Pope John Paul II, in the opening words of his 1999 *Letter to Artists*, gave voice to the experience as this:

"None can sense more deeply than you artists, ingenious creators of beauty that you are, something of the pathos with which God at the dawn of creation looked upon the work of his hands. A glimmer of that feeling has shone so often in your eyes when—like the artists of every age—captivated by the hidden power of sounds and words, colours and shapes, you have admired the work of your inspiration, sensing in it some echo of the mystery of creation with which God, the sole creator of all things, has wished in some way to associate you."

Catholicism and Literature

Catholics are people of the word, convinced of the intrinsic power of language and story. In the Book of Genesis, creation comes forth at God's word. The Gospel of John opens with, "In the beginning was the Word, and the Word was with God, and the Word was God." Week in and week out, Catholics throughout the world gather to celebrate the Eucharist and tell the story of God in prose and poetry, in psalm and song. Our language is sensual and visual. It allows us to explore profound mysteries, understand seemingly incompatible paradox, and contemplate ever-deepening ways of being in the world through the freedom of symbol and metaphor.

Throughout history, Catholic literature has been generated in all possible genres: fiction, poetry, children's works, plays, essays, autobiography, and more. Often prophetic, it makes us pause in our daily routine and see beyond our preconceived boundaries. It may entertain but more often disturbs; it raises more questions than it provides answers. Catholic literature is identified as such, not merely if it is written by a person who is Catholic, but if it employs the history, tradition, culture, theology, and/or spirituality of Catholicism in an informed and meaningful way. In all the myriad variations of style and subject, however, Catholic literature traditionally follows three spiritual themes: Incarnation, sacramentality, and pilgrimage.

Incarnation

The first theme of Catholic literature is incarnationalism. Because we believe that Jesus Christ is fully human and fully divine, Catholic authors do not shy away from all that is truly human. They feel at liberty to describe the depths of evil and sin as well as the heights of goodness and beauty, for both are true of humankind. Graham Greene, in his novel *The Power and the Glory*, tells of a fallen priest, lonely and weak. Yet his very sins and failings allow him to achieve a high degree of sanctity. Flannery O'Connor was known to use shocking and often violent situations in which grace was transformative. Neither of these authors felt the need to gloss over the difficulties, evils, and sufferings of life, rather they pointed the reader to God and God's redeeming grace.

Authors Annie Dillard and Denise Levertov wrote more personally and allow us into their struggle with trials and doubt, paradox and belief. In *Holy the Firm*, Dillard struggles with a God who is love allowing the innocent to suffer. Levertov, who converted to Catholicism late in her life, described the experience of seeing "Paradise in the dust of the street" and a blessed Otherness in the horror and despair (*City Psalm*).

These contemporary authors stand within a long tradition of mystical literature, using symbolic language to depict the struggle of experiencing God's absence at the same time as an intense divine love. Notable among this literature would be thirteenth- and fourteenth-century writings such as *The Cloud of Unknowing*, Julian of Norwich's *Revelations of Divine Love*, and *The Interior Castle* by Saint Teresa of Ávila.

Sacramentality

The second theme of Catholic literature is sacramentality. We believe that God is Creator of the world, revealing himself in and through creation. God dwells with us on earth, animating and transforming everything that exists and, likewise, a sacramental perspective of all creation permeates Catholic literature. All things, events, and experiences "tell" of God and can lead to God.

Though most famously known as an influential philosopher and theologian, Thomas Aquinas was a great poet in this vein who called the universe "a general sacrament which speaks to us of God." The French author, Paul Claudel (1868–1955), wrote of nature as a temple, each part of which possessed a symbolic meaning. Much popular hymnody and numerous meditation videos can be traced to the nineteenth-century British Jesuit priest Gerard Manley Hopkins. His line, "The world is charged with the grandeur of God" has entered popular culture—celebrating nature, the beauty and energy of Christ in all things. Finally, we make mention of John O'Donohue; in 1998, his book *Anam Cara* was published and became an international bestseller. Steeped in Irish Celtic roots, this priest, philosopher, poet, justice advocate died suddenly in 2008 at age 52. His works are still being discovered and released.

Pilgrimage

Saint Augustine of Hippo gave voice to the pilgrimage theme with his familiar lament, "For you have formed us for yourself. Our heart is restless until it rests in you." His fourth-century *Confessions* is the classic tale of one man's journey to God and the internal and external obstacles he battled. Human life is precious, rather than wretched. It is a journey toward a goal and not the goal itself. Widely considered the greatest literary work of the Middle Ages, Dante's *Divine Comedy* is a poetic journey through the realms of the Catholic afterlife—heaven, hell, and purgatory—in an imaginative com-

bination of theology, history, politics, and culture. The *Comedy* was conceived and written while Dante himself was in political exile, hence a painful understanding of exile and longing for return to paradise.

LOVE in Action

- *With which of the mentioned authors are you familiar?*

- *Which of the three themes—Incarnation, sacramentality, pilgrimage—are you drawn toward? Why?*

- *Have you ever written sacred poetry or prose? What was the experience like?*

Catholicism and the Arts

There is often silence when one stands before a sixteen-foot-high block of marble transformed by Michelangelo into the young David. The beauty of human form and the vitality of youth cannot be conveyed in mere words. Likewise, with Michelangelo's *Pieta*, it is as if words would cheapen the profound experience of Mary holding the limp, lifeless body of her Son. This silence speaks loudly; it speaks of the sacred; it speaks of life and anguish and serenity which is simply beyond human comprehension. The *Pieta* and *David* are often referred to as the world's most familiar sculptures. They are part of our tradition of Christian art that is nearly as old as Christianity itself.

The oldest Christian art dates to the beginning of the second century where Christian symbols such as the dove, the fish, the lamb, and the cross decorated the Catacombs of Rome. In the fourth century, the Edict of Milan allowed public Christian worship, thus secret meeting places evolved into large buildings based on the Roman basilica. Altars and aisles began to be richly adorned and religious imagery borrowed heavily from that of the imperial household. Christ was heralded as king; icons of Christ, Mary, and the saints were adorned with halos.

During the Middle Ages and Renaissance, the art of illumination flourished as pages of holy Scripture were written and embellished to enrich the religious experience. Since most people could not read, illustrated stories and religious art were an important channel for handing on the faith. Many Early Renaissance artists, such as Fra Angelico and Botticelli were extremely devout and their art, religious. Fra Angelico filled the walls of his monastery and chapels of Florence with tender devotional frescoes from the life of Jesus. Botticelli was summoned from his workshop in Florence by Pope Sixtus IV to fresco the walls of the Sistine Chapel with strong portrayals of *The Temptations of Christ* and *The Trials of Moses.*

20th-century art has been described as without a mainstream.

This work in the Sistine Chapel ushered in the brief High Renaissance in which artists such as Michelangelo and Raphael worked almost exclusively for the papacy. Marble and bronze, mosaic and fresco—they were all monumental in scope and grandeur. Pope Julius II reigned from 1503–1513 and was determined that Rome would return to the glory of former days. With his wealth of visionary ideas, Julius devised an overall plan which included the Vatican Museum and building a new basilica of St. Peter. The immensity and richness of the art within the Vatican can best be revealed in the words of Emeritus Pope Benedict XVI in his general audience at Castel Gandolfo on August 21, 2011: "It is like a door opened to the infinite."

The vast papal artistic mission was funded partially through the selling of Indulgences, a practice which provoked Martin Luther to the writing of his Ninety-Five Theses in 1517. The Protestant Reformation set off a holocaust of art in many parts of Europe that lasted until the mid-seventeenth century. It was a time with few religious artworks or artists, with the exception of prints and illustrations following scriptural themes. Some painters turned to nature to convey the sacred; others chose images of people caught up in anguish or mystery.

In the seventeenth and eighteenth centuries, European missionary efforts set off a synthesis of European and indigenous styles of religious art. As a response to the increasing secularization of modern life, the nineteenth century saw a search for new religious symbols. For example, Vincent Van Gogh left his preparation as a minister and poured his religious fervor into sunflowers, starry nights, and simple people living in harmony with nature. Immigrants to the United States sought to reconstruct the steeples and statues of their homeland in this foreign soil. They treasure those historical works of art still.

The twentieth-century artistic stream has been described as without a mainstream, but flowing deeply and broadly into the ocean. It may also be said of art in the early years of this twenty-first century that Catholicism is understood as truly universal (its meaning). We are a diverse people, crossing borders of language and culture several times a day. Yet a sleek curve of marble or a sharp glimmer of glass can still draw our attention. A splash of vivid color or the trace of muted pastels can still soften our hearts. We yearn for mystery and are touched by beauty.

Emeritus Pope Benedict XVI referred to God as the Supreme Beauty and invited us to journey the "*via pulchritudinis*"—the "way of beauty"—by means of the great gift of sacred art.

LOVE in Action

- *What is your favorite painting, sculpture, or other piece of sacred art? How do you experience God through it?*

- *What period of Catholic art do you find most intriguing? Why do you think that is?*

- *Have you ever created a work of art? If so, what was the experience like?*

Artistic Periods in Church History

Early Christian art (AD 0–330): Early Christian art was fairly unintelligible, as it was meant to be understood solely by Christians within a persecuted Church. Christians used symbols such as the dove, fish, and lamb, and they depicted Jesus as the Good Shepherd and the evangelists as beasts. The oldest known sculptures came from coffins that first appeared in the second century.

Byzantine and Orthodox art (330–1453): Byzantine art commenced with the Edict of Milan in the early 300s and the dedication of Constantinople as the capital of the Roman Empire by emperor Constantine in 330. It ended with the fall of Constantinople in 1453. The artwork of this era developed out of the Holy Roman Empire. Orthodox art from this same period had its origins east of Rome, deriving from Eastern Catholicism.

Middle Ages (500–1400): During this period, Christianity dominated much of the Western world, resulting in rich pieces of art representing different places and periods: Celtic, Carolingian, Romanesque, and Gothic.

Early and High Renaissance (1430–1550): Beginning in Florence, Italy, this movement, meaning "rebirth," sought to rediscover classical sources. Artwork in this period included masterpieces from artists such as Fra Angelico, Botticelli, Michelangelo, Leonardo da Vinci, and Raphael.

Baroque art (1600–1750): Following the Council of Trent (1545–1563), Christian art became more conservative in order to meet council requirements. Caravaggio and Bernini produced magnificent pieces, some of which were regarded controversially by Church officials at the time.

Eighteenth century: An art form called Rococo, a secular type of Baroque art, emerged, and more classical Palladian architecture became popular. Religious art decreased in this period.

Nineteenth and twentieth centuries: Art influences during this time period came from Protestant and Catholic faith traditions. The artwork itself steadily became more secular. The Gothic Revival architectural style, which drew its inspiration from medieval architecture, developed in the nineteenth century. Newer art forms began to take shape in the 1900s.

Twenty-first century: What Christians create in this century must still unfold. How might we contribute our artistic gifts to the world?

Catholicism and Music

There is something about being human that just needs to make music. Every culture in every age has expressed the mystery of life by bringing together tone and rhythm. As Catholics, we share the musical tradition of ancient Israel through the Psalms and canticles. The Gospel of Luke includes four songs in the first two chapters alone: Mary sings her *Magnificat*, Zechariah his *Benedictus*; angels fill the heavenly skies with "Gloria" at the birth of the Child, and Simeon sings a song of peace at the end of his days. In Matthew's conclusion of the Last Supper, Jesus and his disciples sang a hymn; in Paul's exhortation to the Colossians, they are told to sing "psalms, hymns, and spiritual songs with gratitude in your hearts to God" (Colossians 3:16). In our modern times, Emeritus Pope Benedict referred to sacred music as an integral contribution to New Evangelization. Sacred music is simply part of our lives.

Throughout history, the Church has always been influential in the development of music. Gregorian chant of the fifth and sixth centuries has been called a "sung Bible" because its texts primarily came from Hebrew and Christian Testaments. Chant was learned by ear and committed to memory. It was performed without instrumentation; the melodies were meant to serve the text and inspire spiritual growth. The hauntingly beautiful requiem hymn *Dies Irae* (Day of Wrath) was incorporated into works by Mozart and Verdi. The simple, familiar *Ubi Caritas et amor* (Where charity and love prevail) is thought by some scholars to be a text used in early Christian gatherings. Though Gregorian chant reached its peak in the latter part of the medieval period, it remains a central part of our liturgical and spiritual lives.

During the Middle Ages, composers began to add another melodic line to the single line of chant. Likewise, craftsmen experimented with an instrument that combined wind instruments with stringed instruments and thus was born the organ. The Catholic Church encouraged and commissioned many of the great Renaissance artists such as Bach, Haydn, and Handel, who composed beautiful Masses, chorales, cantatas, and sacred hymns for performance in the cathedral and concert hall alike. The drive with which Mozart labored to complete his *Requiem* was portrayed dramatically in the movie *Amadeus*. The triumphant majesty with which a large choir, accompanied by full orchestra, sings, "Blessed is he who comes in the name of the Lord" rouses even the most weary at Christmas Midnight Mass. The ease with which an ecumenical gathering can jubilantly sing, "Joyful, joyful we adore thee" to the music of Beethoven's Ninth Symphony is as formative as any study or lecture about Christian unity.

Gregorian chant has been referred to as the "sung Bible."

Though a place of honor will always be accorded to Gregorian chant and the organ, sacred music evolves and responds to the spirit of the particular times and culture of those gathered; God's abundant grace continues to overflow. The reforms of the Second Vatican Council called for a wider use of the vernacular language in the Mass, and this included music. A great deal of the Catholic liturgical music of the 1970s was inspired by the contemporary music of the day, which used guitars and folk music style. The Catholic Charismatic movement contributed "praise and worship" music into liturgical settings. By the 1990s and into the early twenty-first century, our contemporary music began to reflect the universal nature of Catholicism with music from many different cultures and sung in many different languages.

Whether it is Gregorian chant or polyphonic choirs, folk guitars or grand organs, music will always be nourishment for our souls and an overflowing expression of our gratitude.

LOVE in Action

• *What is your favorite spiritual hymn or song? What are your memories around it?*

• *Have you ever listened to (or performed in) one of the classical religious masterpieces such as Handel's* Messiah *or a setting of the Mass by Bach, Haydn, or Schubert?*

• *When you realize the impact the Catholic Church has had on music throughout the centuries, what are your thoughts and feelings?*

Concluding Prayer:
Conclude the lesson by praying this version of Psalm 150 antiphonally:

All　Praise the LORD!
Praise God in his sanctuary;
praise him in his mighty
firmament!

Side 1　Praise him for his mighty deeds;
Praise him according to his
surpassing greatness!

Side 2　Praise him with trumpet sound;
Praise him with lute and harp!

Side 1　Praise him with tambourine
and dance;
Praise him with strings
and pipe!

Side 2　Praise him with clanging
cymbals;
Praise him with loud
clashing cymbals!

All　Let everything that breathes
praise the LORD!
Praise the LORD!

SUGGESTED RESOURCES:

Atkinson, Kathleen OSB. *God Is Always There* (Liguori Publications, 2012).

Atkinson, Kathleen OSB. *Letting Go and Letting God* (Liguori Publications, 2013).

Blessed Pope John Paul II. *Letter to Artists* (Liturgy Training Publications, 1999).

Emeritus Pope Benedict XVI. *Letter on the 100th Anniversary of the Pontifical Institute of Sacred Music. Libreria Editrice Vaticana*, 2011.

Haydu, Mark LC, STL. *Meditations on Vatican Art* (Liguori Publications, 2013).

Lysik, David, ed. *The Liturgy Documents: A Parish Resource* (Liturgy Training Publications, 2004). (See *Constitution on the Sacred Liturgy, Music in Catholic Worship, Liturgical Music Today, Environment and Art in Catholic Worship*).

Paintner, Christine Valters. *The Artist's Rule: Nurturing Your Creative Soul With Monastic Wisdom* (Sorin Books, 2011).

Reichardt, Mary. *Encyclopedia of Catholic Literature* (Greenwood Press, 2004).

The Saint John's Bible: In 1998, Saint John's Abbey and University, Collegeville, Minnesota, commissioned renowned calligrapher Donald Jackson to produce a handwritten, hand-illuminated Bible. This work of art unites an ancient Benedictine tradition with the technology and vision of today, illuminating the word of God for a new millennium. Resources for reflection and education abound. Contact: www.saintjohnsbible.org.

Van Parys, Johan PhD. *Symbols That Surround Us: Faithful Reflections* (Liguori Publications, 2012).

CINEMA CONNECTION

Les Misérables (2012), starring Hugh Jackman, Russell Crowe, Anne Hathaway, Amanda Seyfried. Victor Hugo's novel *Les Misérables* is taken from stage to cinema in this musical about the struggles leading to the French Revolution.

ABOUT THE AUTHOR

Kathleen Atkinson, OSB is a Benedictine sister from the Annunciation Monastery in Bismarck, North Dakota. She is a nationally recognized leader in hunger and homelessness education and has developed service learning experiences for all age groups as well as led service teams to a variety of international and United States locations. After returning from Guatemala with the Institute for Trafficked, Exploited and Missing Persons, she is currently engaged in speaking, writing, and a "Ministry on the Margins" with at-risk youth, state penitentiary inmates, and other people who are God's *anawim* among us.

Notes

SESSION 8

Work, Economy, and Politics

By Marie D. Hoff, PhD

Preparation

Have ready a Bible, a candle, matches, and a cross or Christian icon. Set these up on a small table in front of the room where the group will meet, or in the center if you are using a circle format.

Optional

Prepare some simple refreshments for the group to share either before or after the session.

Have music playing quietly in the background on a CD or iPod as participants arrive and settle in.

Opening TEN MINUTES

When everyone is seated, light the candle. Begin with the suggested opening song or use one of your choosing. Or you can go directly to the opening prayer found in the session and have everyone read it aloud together.

Scripture Reading

1 Corinthians 12:1–12

Ask a member of the group to read, or you can read it aloud to the group. Once the passage is read, direct the group members to silently reflect for a minute or two on what they have just heard. This also serves as a centering and quieting exercise for participants.

Supporting Church-document quotes for Session Eight

"Justice is the moral virtue that consists in the constant and firm will to give their due to God and neighbor. Justice toward God is called the 'virtue of religion.' Justice toward men disposes one to respect the rights of each and to establish in human relationships the harmony that promotes equity with regard to persons and the common good" (CCC 1807).

"Goods of production—material or immaterial—such as land, factories, practical or artistic skills, oblige their possessors to employ them in ways that will benefit the greatest number. Those who hold goods for use and consumption should use them with moderation, reserving the better part for guests, for the sick and the poor" (CCC 2405).

"Work represents a fundamental dimension of human existence as participation not only in the act of creation but also in that of redemption. Those who put up with the difficult rigours of work in union with Jesus cooperate, in a certain sense, with the Son of God in his work of redemption and show that they are disciples of Christ bearing his cross, every day, in the activity they are called to do. In this perspective, work can be considered a means of sanctification and an enlivening of earthly realities with the Spirit of Christ" (Compendium of the Social Doctrine of the Church 263).

Work, Economy, and Politics

ALLOW FIFTEEN MINUTES FOR EACH SECTION.

Take a few minutes for the group to read through the section, then move to the **LOVE in Action** questions. Allow each person a minute or two to contribute, and give each group member the opportunity to speak.

Additional questions for reflection and discussion

- *How can Catholics help one another to better see and live an integral relationship between work and the expression of our faith? How can we better enliven earthly realities with the "Spirit of Christ?"*

- *What are some of the practical challenges and obstacles that impede participants' ability to realize the sacredness, the holiness, of their work? Do they feel support or criticism when they attempt to speak and act for justice, fairness, and honesty in their workplaces?*

- *What are the practical implications of the Church's teaching that legitimate government participates in God's authority? In light of political conflict in our own society, what are some ways we can we work for "better" government, rather than "bigger" or "smaller" government? How does the idea of subsidiarity help solve objections to "big" government?*

- *What is the meaning of the Church's constant call to work for the common good? What are the obstacles (moral, economic, political) to providing jobs for everyone who can and wants to work, even people with disabilities?*

- *How does lack of jobs and income contribute to social unrest and personal suffering? How does this offend against the belief in the one body of Christ?*

Closing Rite

FIVE MINUTES

Invite participants to take part in a few moments of silence, then conclude the lesson by reading, from your Bible, Mark 12:28–34 (the two great commandments).

Ask participants for spontaneous prayer.

When finished you can offer this brief blessing to the group:

The LORD bless you and keep you!

The LORD let his face shine upon you, and be gracious to you!

The LORD look upon you kindly and give you peace! (Numbers 6: 24–26)

Concluding Prayer: Good and gracious God, you create and sustain the universe with infinite love. We are privileged to participate in your work by generously using the gifts you have given us to be good stewards of creation and to serve the needs of other people. Grant that we may willingly join our workplace challenges and hardships with the saving work of Christ for the redemption of the whole world. Give us courage and understanding to speak and act for justice in our own society and for all humanity. May we find holiness in our work and help bring all of creation to your kingdom of love and justice, where your Holy Spirit brings fulfillment and lasting joy. We ask these blessings in Jesus' name. Amen.

Work, Economy, and Politics

By Marie D. Hoff, PhD

WHO do we learn from about the meaning of human work?

WHAT are the reasons that human work is a sacred activity?

WHERE do we learn about the Church's teachings on economic and political concerns?

WHEN should Catholics act for social and economic justice?

WHY do people need to find a balance between work and other life activities?

Opening Song: "Lord of all Hopefulness," by Jan Struther, or a hymn of your choice

Opening Prayer: It helps, now and then, to step back and take a long view. The kingdom is not only beyond our efforts, it is even beyond our vision. We accomplish in our lifetime only a tiny fraction of the magnificent enterprise that is God's work....We may never see the end results, but that is the difference between the master builder and the worker. We are workers, not master builders; ministers, not messiahs. We are prophets of a future not our own. Amen. (This prayer is from a reflection attributed to martyred Archbishop Oscar Romero of El Salvador. Copyright USCCB: "Archbishop Oscar Romero Prayer: A Step Along the Way.")

Reading: 1 Corinthians 12:1–12 (spiritual gifts)

Spend a moment in quiet reflection.

Working for the Common Good

When the teachers of the law came to test Jesus, to find out if he really knew God's law handed down through Moses, they had to admit he perfectly understood its essence—to strive toward perfect love of both God and neighbor. Jesus further taught that we can only demonstrate our true love for God in the care and concern we take toward our neighbor. In essence, we will be judged by our work to care for the "least" among us (see especially the majestic story of the Last Judgment in Matthew 25:31–40).

Jesus' ministry of teaching and healing, and his suffering, death, and resurrection were for all people. Through him we learn that our neighbor is truly the entire human family, most especially those we encounter in our daily lives. Our religious beliefs and values help us find meaning and purpose throughout our days. Besides through our families and close friends, the most important arenas in which Christian values endow our lives with meaning and purpose are the workplace and in the practice of responsible citizenship.

"Going to work" is a major and a necessary activity of life for adults. Here our love of God and neighbor is expressed, not so much by personal affection, but by our practice of workplace justice and community. As citizens, we express love of neighbor by participating, according to our abilities, to ensure justice in public laws and policies for all people, especially for the most vulnerable and poor.

Spirituality of Work

As Catholics, we believe human work is genuinely holy when it expresses love and justice toward others. The holiness of human work is rooted in the story of creation in the Book of Genesis: God worked for six days declaring all things "good." Human persons, male and female, created on the last day, were pronounced as especially good, as we have been made in the very "image of God."

Work is holy, first and foremost, because through work we imitate and share in the joyous creativity of God. Our work allows us to become the very hands and heart of God, and to keep God's creative action going through time. When we raise and teach a child, grow a crop, build a house, counsel a distressed person, research and work for ways to promote peace, cure diseases, and ensure clean water and responsible agriculture (or meet any other legitimate human need), we are continuing God's work of creation.

Secondly, work is sacred because through work we carry out God's command to practice stewardship, to care for and use the goods of the earth responsibly and respectfully. As earthly creatures ourselves, with bodies that need food, clothing, and shelter, we are permitted to use, but not abuse, the other good things God created. Work expresses our great dignity as human persons when we use the goods of the earth responsibly to meet our own needs and the needs of others.

Human work is genuinely holy when it expresses love and justice toward others.

Stewardship includes the right and duty to develop our God-given gifts. By using our talents and increasing our skills to serve the genuine needs of other people, we fulfill our human potential, achieve holiness and glorify God. Pope John Paul II taught that work has dignity because the one doing the work is a human person.

The holiness and sacredness of our work is grounded in the life, death, and teachings of Jesus. "Enfleshed" (incarnate) in earthly existence, God-Made-Man reinforces the importance of life on earth. In his hidden life as a carpenter and his public ministry of healing and teaching about the coming of God's kingdom, Jesus sets an example to emphasize for us the value of human work that with him becomes an important ministry of love and service to other people.

The Bible recognizes the sufferings that come with human work. The Book of Genesis represents the hardships of work as a punishment for sin. Nevertheless, the Bible as a whole condemns workplace hardships that come through unjust relationships. The prophets denounce injustice (oppressing workers and cheating them of just wages) as a form of idolatry and blasphemy against God. James (5:1–6) exhorts the payment of just wages, and Paul instructs constantly for genuine love and brotherly relationships between members of the Christian communities. It is Paul who gives to Christians a holy meaning and noble purpose for the hardships, challenges, and even injustices of life and work; by them we share in the sufferings and redemptive work of Christ: "Bear one another's burdens, and so you will fulfill the law of Christ....let us do good to all, but especially to those who belong to the family of the faith" (Galatians 6:2; 10).

"Work can be a means of sanctification and a way of animating earthly realities with the Spirit of Christ" (*CCC* 2427).

LOVE in Action

- *Describe how you see the relationship between your work and your faith?*

- *Share an experience where you chose to stand up for justice, either in your workplace or as a citizen.*

- *How does the biblical call to stewardship help guide your actions?*

Work and Economic Justice Today

"...The Church is not bound to any particular economic, political, or social system; it has lived with many forms of economic and social organization and will continue to do so, evaluating each according to moral and ethical principles: What is the impact of the system on people? Does it support or threaten human dignity?" (*Pastoral Letter on U.S. Economy*, paragraph 130, page 66).

In modern times, vast changes were wrought in society through political, industrial, and scientific revolutions. Working conditions in factories and mines for men, women, and even very young children were truly horrifying: They degraded human dignity, kept people in poverty, and led to early death. Such gross injustices still persist in some parts of the world. In our own country, significant levels of poverty and unemployment persist. Since the nineteenth century, Church leaders have taught about the religious and moral dimensions of human work. Popes have addressed economic and political systems through social encyclicals (public letters), and bishops in various regions of the world have issued pastoral letters.

In 1986, the U.S. Conference of Catholic Bishops issued an important and beautiful pastoral letter addressing justice issues in the American economy and workplace. This document distilled many key ideas from 125 years of Church teachings and applied them to our experience of work and economy in the United States. Its insights and recommendations remain deeply relevant to present circumstances in our country, including our economic and political relationship to other countries.

We achieve holiness through observing "ethical norms" (*Pastoral Letter*, pages 32–49) that include both our workplace responsibilities and our workplace rights. As employees, we are bound to work to our full ability and cooperate with others to develop the product or service efficiently and effectively. Even more importantly, workplace cooperation creates genuine community in the workplace. The right of workers to form unions (associations) in order to participate in decisions that affect their lives has always been affirmed by the Church. Because of human dignity, people have a right to associate with others to promote community and human solidarity as well as to pursue their mutual economic interests. The U.S. bishops frequently call on unions to re-envision their essential role (along with managers, owners, and government) in revitalizing jobs and strengthening economic functioning. It is noteworthy that the Constitution of the United States also supports this right of "association," without naming workplace unions, *per se.* Perhaps the most fundamental economic justice right every person has is the right to have a job—to have a place in the world of work: "Unemployment is a tragedy no matter whom it strikes, but the tragedy is compounded by the unequal and unfair way it is distributed in our society" (*Economic Justice for All*, 1986).

> *"Unemployment is a tragedy that is compounded by the unequal...way it is distributed."*
> U.S. CATHOLIC BISHOPS

This is a complex and difficult problem, but all sectors of society—labor, government, citizens, and corporate owners—must take responsibility to move toward the goal of work for all who are able, and economic security for everyone especially the young, the old, and the disabled. Individual flourishing, family life, and social peace depend on it. Working toward this goal is truly a way of building up in love the one body of Christ, of believing in human solidarity as taught by Pope John Paul II, and of living the truth in charity as taught by Emeritus Pope Benedict XVI. We love others by ensuring they have a voice and a share in the human family's work.

As an employer, we are ethically bound to pay living wages, to provide a safe and healthy work environment, including reasonable working hours so workers can also fulfill their duties to family and community, with time for rest and worship. Employers have a right to expect good work, honesty, and cooperation from their employees. When people cooperate responsibly to respect each other's rights, the workplace contributes toward the common good of society and enables people to meet genuine human needs, achieve their full human potential, and thus become holy. In this ideal vision, we truly worship and honor God and love our neighbor through our daily work.

As Catholics, we strongly value family life and recognize the task of raising children as also being real work. The Church asks society to support the essential contribution of family life and child-rearing to build up a strong and well-functioning society through its support for two major public policy directives: (1) living wage policies that prevent degrading levels of poverty which put marriages and children at grave risk; and (2) workplace policies for "time off" (for regular weekly rest, sick leave, and annual vacations) that enable parents to build family togetherness, engage in Sunday worship, and pursue relationships with friends and the poor and lonely in our community.

Perhaps we can ask ourselves if we obey the Third Commandment "to keep holy the sabbath day" or if we have become "workaholics" and "shopaholics" with very little time for genuine leisure as described above. As Catholics, we believe work is central and important to human life and community, but we also believe we must find a balance with other important aspects of living a holy life. If we begin to make a consistent effort to renew our observance of the Lord's Day we may notice a greater peacefulness in ourselves, relief from the stress of constant work and shopping. And we might contribute to the same for low-income workers who must cater to people's shopping or recreational demands seven days a week. In short, the Church encourages balance between work and other life activities.

It certainly is wonderful if we can take short breaks at our job to say a prayer and be aware of the presence of God, but the holiness of our work does not depend on this opportunity. Work is redemptive and sanctifying (*CCC* 2427) when done with love, justice, and intention for genuine service to the larger community...."Work should enable the working person to become 'more a human being' more capable of acting intelligently, freely, and in ways that lead to self-realization" (*Economic Justice for All*).

LOVE in Action

- *What can you do to improve balance in your life between work and leisure?*
- *How might you try to make your daily work more of genuine service to others?*
- *What keeps us from ensuring jobs for everyone?*

The Church Engages With the World

In the Gospel of Luke (20:25), Jesus tells us to give to Caesar (the worldly ruler) what is Caesar's and to God what is God's. This saying has been sometimes misinterpreted to mean an absolute separation between religion and politics, between the Church and the world. Throughout the history of Christianity the Church has struggled to find the proper balance, the proper relationship between Church and state, between religion and the daily life of work, economy, and politics. Saint Augustine wrote his famous book *The City of God* to explore these connections. With Augustine, we believe the city of God (God's kingdom, God's rule) exists and grows within the city of the world, but is not identical with it. In the Gospel parable of the wheat and the weeds (Matthew 13:24–30; 36–43), Jesus says to let the weeds exist until the harvest when the good will be separated from the bad. One way to interpret this parable is to understand that as Christians we live within a sinful world in order to transform it through our practices of love and justice; we are not called to run away from the world but to infuse Christian values into economic and political structures of our day.

Catholics reject sectarianism (withdrawal from the world into purist, isolated groups) as well as theocracy (complete integration between religion and secular governance). In the documents of Vatican II, particularly Pastoral Constitution on the Church in the Modern World (*Gaudium et Spes*), the Church calls for engagement with the world. As Catholic Christians, we share in the "joy and the hope, the grief and the anguish" of all people, particularly of those who are "poor or afflicted in any way" (from Pastoral Constitution on the Church in the Modern World).

The Church engages with the world through relationships with secular governance entities in a variety of ways. The Church does so by teaching that good government legitimately participates in the authority of God. Government has a necessary and proper authority to regulate economic activity for the protection of workers, the poor and vulnerable, and the natural environment. As Catholics, we do not subscribe to the so-called "night watchman" view of government with only the most minimalist duties to protect life and property. On the contrary, we believe government is one of several arenas in which people come together to form community, meet human needs, and promote stability and order for the common good of everyone in society. Neither "big" government nor "small" government is desired, but rather "good" government in which justice for all (the common good) takes precedence over other social goals.

On the other extreme, based on experience with totalitarian governments (especially Naziism and communism), the Church sees that government can become oppressive or coldly bureaucratic, violating basic human dignity. To check the capacity of government to "take over" people's lives, Catholic social-justice teachings have three major tools in the "idea-box": (1) people's right to participate in decision-making, (2) the right to own private property, and (3) the principle of subsidiarity—to guide government action.

The Church affirms the rights and duties of workers to participate in decisions in the workplace. In their pastoral letter on the U.S. economy, the bishops also stress the duties of citizens to active, democratic involvement in civic life so that government properly fulfills its role to promote justice and the common good of all.

Our right to private property exists to promote basic human dignity, protect family life, and instill economic motivation to work. However, property ownership, especially of economic, productive resources, is not absolute or unlimited; it is conditioned on the needs of the whole community.

For protection of human rights and control of socially corrosive accumulation of wealth (private property), Catholics accept the duty of government to actively be the watchdog for: (a) *contractual justice* through regulation of wages, working conditions, and financial transactions; (b) *distributive justice* through fair and equitable taxation. Taxation is a legitimate function of government to limit excessive inequities in wealth and power (which lead to social unrest and violence), to provide for support of the poor and vulnerable in society, and to meet common needs, such as transportation, food and drug safety, environmental protection and other democratically determined purposes; (c) and *social justice* to be directed toward achieving the common good of the whole society.

> "A society that wishes and intends to remain at the service of the human being on every level is a society that has the common good—the good of all people and of the whole person—as its primary goal. The human person cannot find fulfillment in himself, that is, apart from the fact that he exists 'with' others' and 'for' others" (*Compendium of the Social Doctrine of the Church*, Pontifical Council for Justice and Peace, 2004, paragraph 165).

Subsidiarity is the third tool to control government's tendency to "take over." In brief, subsidiarity means higher or larger units of society, such as state or federal government, should not replace or totally control lower or smaller units of society, such as family, neighborhood, and civic organizations. Neither should larger-scale political units completely abandon or ignore local, small-scale groups. Rather, through protective and supportive laws, cooperative partnerships, and financial support, government should subsidize genuine, face-to-face forms of community.

Some examples: By laws and financial incentives, government can support parents' ability to stay at home for child-rearing during the crucial early years; police departments can work cooperatively with neighborhood associations to involve people in the safety and upkeep of their own local communities; state and federal governments can assist Church organizations, such as Catholic Charities, to expand services to vulnerable children, refugees, homeless or unemployed people.

The Church engages with the world of work and secular governance through advocacy for human dignity and social justice in public policy making. As ethical teacher the Church must point out justice and injustice

in proposed laws and programs and advocate for unmet needs. As individual lay Catholics, we participate in this advocacy by joining our voices and our efforts with others through our parishes, our diocese or other Catholic organizations, and through our own civic participation in justice advocacy. As an organization, the Church advocates around public policy (including international justice issues) through the Office for Social Development and World Peace at the U.S. Conference of Catholic Bishops in Washington, D.C. Catholic Charities, Catholic Relief Services, and many other Catholic organizations also provide opportunities to participate in group advocacy pertaining to various social needs and concerns.

The Church engages the world by teaching and encouraging Catholics to study the social-justice teachings of the Church that have been developed over the past 125 years to apply the Gospel to the modern world of economics and politics. We engage the world and practice our faith in our daily activities by being good citizens and by conducting ourselves honorably and earnestly in the workplace to infuse Christian virtues of justice, fairness, and respect for human dignity. Lay Catholics with knowledge and expertise in specific areas, for example, financial regulation, job creation, or social welfare services, engage the world when they consider how Catholic social-justice values apply in their field of work, whether as skilled public or private employees or as elected government representatives.

Conclusion

Catholics respect secular activity as important in its own right. But we do not believe in an absolute wall of separation between religion and the work of politics and other secular activity. Religious values should infuse our activity, but most likely, we are unable to pray explicitly while we concentrate on the task before us. It's during our dedicated prayer and reflection time where we examine the purposes for which we act in our "worldly" activities: do we work primarily for power, fame, and material benefits (the three temptations of Jesus in the desert), or do we choose our work out of a genuine concern to serve other people? Prayer and reflection time, that is, listening for the voice of God, can help us set our intentions and understand how we can more faithfully carry out the two great commandments to love God and love neighbor. Prayer, reflection, study, and conversation with others can help us see how our daily work and civic involvement contributes to spreading Jesus' Good News of the coming of God's kingdom (God's reign) in the world.

LOVE in Action

- *How do you go about trying to be a good citizen?*
- *What have you learned about the connection between faith and daily life?*
- *What does the idea of the common good mean to you?*

Concluding Prayer: Good and gracious God, you create and sustain the universe with infinite love. We are privileged to participate in your work by generously using the gifts you have given us to be good stewards of creation and to serve the needs of other people. Grant that we may willingly join our workplace challenges and hardships with the saving work of Christ for the redemption of the whole world. Give us courage and understanding to speak and act for justice in our own society and for all humanity. May we find holiness in our work and help bring all of creation to your kingdom of love and justice, where your Holy Spirit brings fulfillment and lasting joy. We ask these blessings in Jesus' name. Amen.

SUGGESTED RESOURCES:

Hoff, Marie D. PhD. *Happy the People: When Love Becomes Justice* (Liguori Publications, 2013).

Hudock, Barry. *Faith Meets World: The Gift and Challenge of Catholic Social Teaching* (Liguori Publications, 2013).

Pope Leo XIII. *Libreria Editrice Vaticana. Rerum Novarum,* 1891.

United States Conference of Catholic Bishops. *Economic Justice for All,* 1986.

CINEMA CONNECTION

Entertaining Angels: The Dorothy Day Story (1996), starring Moira Kelly, Martin Sheen, Lenny von Dohlen. Dorothy Day spent much of her life praying for and working with the poor. This film highlights her work, social activism, and the events that led up to and sustained the Catholic Worker movement.

ABOUT THE AUTHOR

Marie D. Hoff, PhD, received her doctorate in social welfare and has taught social policy for thirteen years at the graduate and undergraduate levels. She spent five years developing a Catholic Charities agency for the state of Idaho, including educating and assisting parishes to become involved in both charitable and social-justice work. Through the years, she has given numerous lectures and workshops, directed services to clients, and planned programs and volunteer community work for social concerns.

Notes

SESSION
9

Discernment

By James Kubicki, SJ

Preparation

Have ready a Bible, a candle, matches, and a cross or Christian icon. Set these up on a small table in front of the room where the group will meet, or in the center if you are using a circle format.

Optional

Prepare some simple refreshments for the group to share either before or after the session.

Have music playing quietly in the background on a CD or iPod as participants arrive and settle in.

Opening *TEN MINUTES*

When everyone is seated, light the candle. Begin with the suggested opening song or use one of your choosing. Or you can go directly to the opening prayer found in the session and have everyone read it aloud together.

Scripture Reading

1 Kings 3:4–14

Ask a member of the group to read, or you can read it aloud to the group. Once the passage is read, direct the group members to silently reflect for a minute or two on what they have just heard. This also serves as a centering and quieting exercise for participants.

Supporting catechism quotes for Session Nine

"The desire for God is written in the human heart, because man is created by God and for God; and God never ceases to draw man to himself....'The dignity of man rests above all on the fact that he is called to communion with God....For if man exists, it is because God has created him through love, and through love continues to hold him in existence'" (CCC 27); GS 19.

"Prayer and Christian life are inseparable, for they concern the same love and the same renunciation, proceeding from love; the same filial and loving conformity with the Father's plan of love; the same transforming union in the Holy Spirit who conforms us more and more to Christ Jesus; the same love for all men, the love with which Jesus has loved us....He 'prays without ceasing' who unites prayer to works and good works to prayer. Only in this way can we consider as realizable the principle of praying without ceasing" (CCC 2745); John 15:16–17; Origen, De orat. 12: PG 11, 452c.

"By a discernment according to the Spirit, Christians have to distinguish between the growth of the Reign of God and the progress of the culture and society in which they are involved. This distinction is not a separation. Man's vocation to eternal life does not suppress, but actually reinforces, his duty to put into action in this world the energies and means received from the Creator to serve justice and peace" (CCC 2820); see GS 22; 32; 39; 45; EN 31.

Discernment

ALLOW FIFTEEN MINUTES FOR EACH SECTION.

Take a few minutes for the group to read through the section, then move to the **LOVE in Action** questions. Allow each person a minute or two to contribute, and give each group member the opportunity to speak.

Additional questions for reflection and discussion

- *Who are some examples of faith in your life? Those among the saints? Why are you drawn to these examples?*

- *Consider the depth of God's love for you. How might you engage God's love this week? What are some ways you can share it with others?*

- *Think of a time when you have had to discern the path before you. Did you ask God for guidance? Share your experience.*

Closing Rite

FIVE MINUTES

Invite participants to take part in a few moments of silence, then conclude the lesson by reading Philippians 4:8–9:

Finally, brothers, whatever is true, whatever is honorable, whatever is just, whatever is pure, whatever is lovely, whatever is gracious, if there is any excellence and if there is anything worthy of praise, think about these things.

Keep on doing what you have learned and received and heard and seen in me. Then the God of peace will be with you.

Ask the participants for spontaneous prayer.

When finished, you can offer this brief blessing to the group:

The LORD bless you and keep you!

The LORD let his face shine upon you, and be gracious to you!

The LORD look upon you kindly and give you peace! (Numbers 6: 24–26)

Concluding Prayer: Loving God, you are very near. Your Spirit is as close to us as our breath. May your Spirit help us to discern the ways that you are speaking through the people and events of our lives. As we listen, may we always pay attention to your inspirations and follow them as they lead us to the perfect happiness and peace for which you created each of us. Amen.

9

Discernment

By James Kubicki, SJ

*

WHO is God in relationship to me?

WHAT spiritual exercises assist us to discern the will of God?

WHERE do we experience God?

WHEN ought we to discern God's will?

WHY should we discern movements in our spiritual and physical lives?

Opening Song: "They'll Know We Are Christians by Our Love," by Peter Scholtes, or a hymn of your choice

Opening Prayer: Father, you sent Jesus as the true and perfect revelation of your love. He is the way that leads us to fulfill our purpose, who brings us to perfect happiness. Send your Spirit to help us to discern the particular ways in which Jesus wants to lead us individually so that we may be united with you and in the communion of saints forever. Amen.

Reading: 1 Kings 3:4–14 (Solomon's Prayer for Wisdom)

Spend a moment in quiet reflection.

The Meaning of Life

Victor Frankl (1905–1997) was an Austrian psychiatrist who studied under the two great therapists of his time—Sigmund Freud, who saw humanity's basic need as the pursuit of pleasure, and Alfred Adler, who saw humanity's basic drive as the desire for power. Frankl worked with patients during the Great Depression of the 1930s. In losing everything financially, his patients had lost their sense of purpose, their desire to live. When the Nazis gained control of Austria, Frankl, being Jewish, was sent with this family to various work and concentration camps. Being an observer of human behavior, he wondered why—all things such as age, health, strength being equal—some people survived and others wasted away and died. He concluded that humanity's most basic need was not pleasure or power but purpose and meaning. It wasn't enough to survive the camps simply for the sake of survival. There had to be a purpose or meaning that transcended the individual. Some survived for religious reasons, others for their family, others because they were artists and wanted to live in order to bring beauty into an ugly world, and still others because they were scientists whose research would help humanity.

There is a comic strip in which children can ask the cartoonist questions that are on their minds. In most cases they are scientific questions—how things work and why they are the way they are. Recently, one child asked: "What's the meaning of life?" The cartoonist's response was pretty shocking: "The meaning is up to you. And it could mean nothing at all." Is it true that life means nothing at all? Most of us cannot believe that life is meaningless. Frankl's reflections show that life must mean something that is bigger than the individual, otherwise we won't ultimately have the will to survive. And is it true that the meaning is up to each person? Most of us embrace an objective reality that

> *But what is the meaning of life? Why do we exist? What is every person's ultimate purpose in life?*

shows that the meaning of life is not entirely up to the individual. If it were so subjective, people could choose evil things to give their lives meaning—greed, lust, even torture and murder. Needless to say, there is no meaning in sinning.

Life has a true and positive meaning, and its meaning can be known. But what is the meaning of life? Why do we exist? What is every person's ultimate purpose in life? And how do our individual choices and goals help us to attain our ultimate purpose? Discernment involves coming to know our ultimate purpose and then making the choices that help us attain it.

Some examples

In his youth, Saint Ignatius of Loyola (1491–1556) thought that the meaning of life consisted of pleasure, romance, and honor. A battle injury changed all that. Laid up in his family's castle, recovering from a wounded leg, he began reading the only books on hand, spiritual books—the *Life of Christ* and the *Lives of the Saints*. He began to see that the life he had been living lacked meaning, that it really wasn't satisfying. And he began to dream of a different life.

Dorothy Day (1897–1980), whose cause for canonization is under way, went through a similar change. She lived a bohemian lifestyle in Greenwich Village with artists, writers, and socialist radicals. She pursued relationships with men whom she thought would fill her every need, having an affair in which she was pressured to have an abortion but was abandoned anyway. She married a man twice her age and divorced him after a year, tried to resume the affair, and finally entered into a relationship with an anarchist who did not believe in marriage. They had a child, and the experience of motherhood put Dorothy in touch with goodness, beauty, and love. The child changed her life. She remembered how moved she was by the beautiful worship she experienced as a child in the Episcopal Church. She had her daughter baptized a Catholic. In time she entered the Catholic Church, for she saw it as the Church of the poor masses whom she felt called to serve. She separated from her lover and, as a single mother, dedicated herself to helping the poor through writing and direct service.

What brought about the great changes in the lives of Saint Ignatius and Dorothy Day? It was the experience of a deeper love than the ones they had been pursuing.

LOVE in Action

- *Has your understanding of the meaning or purpose of life changed over the years? If so, how?*

- *Organizations often propose writing a mission statement and then determining the goals to achieve that mission and, even more specifically, the strategies for attaining those goals. What is your basic mission in life, and what are some goals and strategies for achieving your mission?*

- *Have you ever experienced a radical change in the direction of your life the way Saint Ignatius or Dorothy Day did? What brought on that change?*

God Who Is Love

A fifth-century Greek bishop, Diadochus of Photice, wrote: "Anyone who loves God in the depths of his heart has already been loved by God. In fact, the measure of a man's love for God depends upon how deeply aware he is of God's love for him." How deep is God's love for you? God's love for us—for you—is without depth or limit. It is infinite. Discernment is really about growing in the awareness of the depths of God's love and responding to it.

According to the First Letter of John, "God is love" (4: 8, 16). If God is love and, according to the Book of Genesis, human beings are "made in the image and likeness of God," then we are made by love and for love. The meaning of our lives is love. We exist to learn to love, and discernment is basically choosing the path by which we can do this.

But what is "love?" Today the word "love" is used for all kinds of things, and many of them are just the opposite of love. We think of love as primarily a feeling, of desire and the pleasure that comes when the desire is fulfilled. We end up "loving" whatever makes us feel good. This understanding of love is false, for it's all about "me."

True love is not so much about getting as giving. We look to God to know the meaning of love. The revelation God has given us is that God is a communion of persons—three persons, one God. This is a great mystery that cannot be discovered through scientific analysis nor ever be completely understood. At the very heart of God there is communion, there is love. This Trinitarian communion of persons is perfectly complete and happy, but it is the nature of love to go out of itself and to share. So God created a world and creatures with whom God could share love. Each individual person has been created because God desires to share love with that person. And every person is unique, giving God the opportunity to love in a unique way and to receive a love from that person that no other person can give.

At the very heart of God there is communion, there is love.

Shortly after his election as pope, Benedict XVI said: "Each of us is the result of a thought of God. Each of us is willed, each of us is loved, each of us is necessary."

The thoughts of God are eternal. It's not as though God thought of you at some moment in time shortly before your conception. God had you in mind from before time, from all eternity. As God said through the prophet Jeremiah, "Before I formed you in the womb I knew you" (1:5).

No one is an accident or a mistake. No matter what the circumstances of your conception, God was present, intending or willing your existence.

We often take our limited experience of love and project it unto God, wondering how God can love or ever be concerned simultaneously with all the billions of people on the face of the earth. Basil the Great offers a beautiful example from nature to help us appreciate God's infinite and individual love. "Like the sunshine, which permeates all the atmosphere, spreading over land and sea, and yet is enjoyed by each person as though it were for him alone, so the Spirit pours forth his grace in full measure, sufficient for all, and yet is present as though exclusively to everyone who can receive him. To all creatures that share in him he gives a delight limited only by their own nature, not by his ability to give." If the sun shines with equal intensity on all the flowers, how much more does the Creator of the sun shine his love with equal intensity on all those made in the divine image, all God's children. God loves each flower in the garden of humanity with an infinite and passionate love, as though each one of us were the only flower.

Each person is necessary to God, otherwise God would not have created that individual. Each person gives God a unique love and joy that no other person can give to God because, in the words of Blessed Pope John Paul II, "each person is unique, precious, and unrepeatable." Every individual returns love to God in a way in which no other person who ever lived or will live can. God has a wonderful and loving plan for creation, and every human being has a special place in that plan.

Ultimately, discerning one's path in life or even making daily choices has to do with responding to the infinite love of God. As the First Letter of John puts it: "In this is love: not that we have loved God, but that he loved us" (4:10). "We love because he first loved us" (4:19). Discernment deals with finding out where and how God wants to love you at any given moment. Knowing this love, the natural response will be to return love. And just as it's natural in human love to share the interests and desires of the beloved, so it is with God. To really love God means loving what and whom God loves—all creation and all God's creatures, humanity, all my brothers and sisters. In fact, according to John in his First Letter, you cannot love God and not love your neighbor: "If anyone says, 'I love God,' but hates his brother, he is a liar; for whoever does not love a brother whom he has seen cannot love God whom he has not seen. This is the commandment we have from him: whoever loves God must also love his brother" (4:20–21).

When a scholar of the law asked Jesus (in the Book of Luke) what must be done to inherit eternal life (to attain the purpose of life), he asked his questioner, "What is written in the law? How do you read it?" The scholar responded: "You shall love the Lord, your God, with all your heart, with all your being, with all your strength, and with all your mind, and your neighbor as yourself." And Jesus replied: "You have answered correctly; do this and you will live." According to Jesus, this is the most basic commandment. It is the way to attain the purpose for which God created us.

LOVE in Action

- *God is love, and humans—made in God's image—are created for love. But what is "love?" How would you define "love?"*

- *What has been your greatest experience of receiving love? What has been your greatest experience of loving another? What has your experience of love taught you about God's love?*

- *How do the two commandments—love God and love your neighbor—really go together and form one single commandment?*

Elements of Discernment

Our purpose in life is to love, but we can only love insofar as we are aware of how deeply we are loved. How do we grow in this awareness? Through prayer. Prayer is the necessary context for discernment. Prayer is time spent with God. Spending time with another—speaking and listening and being silent together—is essential for any relationship. And this is true for our relationship with God as well.

By prayerfully reading the Scriptures we become familiar with God's ways, God's values. In other spiritual readings, especially the biographies of saints and other heroes of our faith, we see how others fulfilled their purpose by loving God and their neighbors.

Saint Ignatius experienced his tremendous change by reading about the lives of the saints. As he lay in bed recovering from surgery, he fantasized about doing brave deeds as a knight and winning the hand of a fair maiden. He also daydreamed about following the paths that Saint Dominic and Saint Francis of Assisi had taken as they followed Christ. He noticed a difference between the effects the two dreams had on him. In his autobiography he wrote (see *The Liturgy of the Hours*):

> "When Ignatius reflected on worldly thoughts, he felt intense pleasure; but when he gave them up out of weariness, he felt dry and depressed. Yet when he thought of living the rigorous sort of life he knew the saints had lived, he not only experienced pleasure when he actually thought about it, but even after he dismissed these thoughts, he still experienced great joy. Yet he did not pay attention to this, nor did he appreciate it until one day, in a moment of insight, he began to marvel at the difference. Then he understood his experience: thoughts of one kind left him sad, the others full of joy. And this was the first time he applied a process of reasoning to his religious experience.

Prayer is time spent with God.

Later on, when he began to formulate his spiritual exercises, he used this experience as an illustration to explain the doctrine he taught his disciples on the discernment of spirits."

Thus Saint Ignatius discovered where true happiness lay and where God wanted to love him.

For Saint Ignatius, discernment at its most basic level involves paying attention to the various movements of the heart—positive and negative, joy or sadness, peace or agitation—and using those interior movements as signposts indicating where God is leading a person to fulfill his or her destiny, his or her unique place in God's plan, his or her own way of loving God and neighbor.

Dorothy Day also reflected on the movements of her heart and followed the path that led to inner peace and joy, even in the midst of suffering. As a child she was drawn to religious practices but later gave them up for an exciting life among literary people and radicals who often viewed religion as childish and counterproductive to social justice. The excitement didn't last. Indeed, it gave way to one disappointment after another until finally, through the child that developed within her and was born, God touched her with a sense of purpose and love that she had never known. She wanted to make sure her daughter knew that deeper love, so she had her baptized. She began praying, and, when the man she was with refused to marry her, she separated from him. Trying to discern how she was to live as a writer and single mother, she met a French immigrant, Peter Maurin. Their commitment to both religion and social justice led them to found the Catholic Worker movement. Dorothy, by paying attention to the deepest movements within her heart, was drawn to love God and her neighbor in a way that has given unique glory and pleasure to God.

Discernment begins as an exercise that makes you aware of how God meets you in the events and people of your daily life. Just as the Bible is the record of God's activity in the lives of nations and individuals, so you can also write your own "scripture," detailing how God has been present in your life. An important part of making good choices involves paying daily attention to the movements of your heart. Like Saint Ignatius reflecting on how his different readings and thoughts affected his interior state, like Dorothy Day discerning the difference between pleasure and joy as she became a mother, so you also need to reflect daily on how things that happen in your day affect your interior state. To discern what God wants for you, you need to review your day to see where God was, how God was calling you, and how you responded.

Saint Ignatius saw such a daily review, which he called an "examen," as so important that he told the Jesuits in the religious order he founded that if the activities of the day precluded other prayer practices, the examen ought never be dropped.

There are various ways in which to make the examen. The simplest approach is to find some time either at the end of the day or at the beginning of a new day, to sit quietly, take a walk, or journal. Begin with a prayer recognizing you are in God's presence, thanking God for your life and all the ways you were blessed during the day you are reviewing, and asking for the help of the Holy Spirit to see yourself with both truth and love, to see yourself as God sees you. Then review the day as though you were watching a video of it, fast-forwarding through less important moments and pausing at those moments where your heart was being moved with negative or positive reactions to the events and people of your day. What was God saying to you through those events and the reactions you felt? How was God affirming you or challenging you through them? How did your choices and deeds help or hinder you in loving God and your neighbor? Then, in closing, thank God for being so present in your day. Ask for forgiveness for the ways that you did not love, for the times that you put yourself before God or your neighbor.

As you reflect upon God's presence in your daily life and the movements of your heart, you will be better able to discern how God is calling you to fulfill your ultimate mission and purpose in life—how you are being called in specific ways to learn to love God and your neighbor. This daily exercise will give you a discerning mind and a heart more attuned to God in whom, according the Bible, "we live and move and have our being" (Acts of the Apostles 17:28).

LOVE in Action

- *What's the difference between "saying prayers" and "praying?"*

- *What has been your experience of spiritual reading? What are some books and/or stories of saints or good people that have helped you?*

- *Saint Ignatius calls the deepest interior movements "consolation" and "desolation." What have been your experiences of these two? How has reflecting on them helped you in making a decision?*

- *How might you write a "scripture of your life?" How different would it be from the biblical Scriptures and in what ways?*

Concluding Prayer: Loving God, you are very near. Your Spirit is as close to us as our breath. May your Spirit help us to discern the ways that you are speaking through the people and events of our lives. As we listen, may we always pay attention to your inspirations and follow them as they lead us to the perfect happiness and peace for which you created each of us. Amen.

SUGGESTED RESOURCES:

Kubicki, James SJ. *A Heart on Fire: Rediscovering Devotion to the Sacred Heart of Jesus* (Ave Maria Press, 2012).

Saint Ignatius of Loyola. *The Spiritual Exercises.*

CINEMA CONNECTION

Schindler's List (1993), starring Liam Neeson, Ben Kingsley, Ralph Fiennes. During World War II, Oskar Schindler becomes concerned over time for his Jewish work force.

ABOUT THE AUTHOR

James Kubicki, SJ, has been the national director of the Apostleship of Prayer since 2003. Presently he travels around the country giving retreats and parish missions, contributing regularly to Catholic radio stations in Phoenix, Lexington (Kentucky), Cincinnati, and Portland (Oregon). He also appears regularly on the Relevant Radio and EWTN Radio Networks. His award-winning book *A Heart on Fire: Rediscovering Devotion to the Sacred Heart of Jesus* was published by Ave Maria Press in 2012. The Apostleship of Prayer website is www.apostleshipofprayer.org.

Liturgy as a Form of Community Prayer and Manifestation of God's Love

....

By Emily Strand, MA

Preparation

Have ready a Bible, a candle, matches, and a cross or Christian icon. Set these up on a small table in front of the room where the group will meet, or in the center if you are using a circle format.

Optional

Prepare some simple refreshments for the group to share either before or after the session.

Have music playing quietly in the background on a CD or iPod as participants arrive and settle in.

Opening *TEN MINUTES*

When everyone is seated, light the candle. Begin with the suggested opening song or use one of your choosing. Or you can go directly to the opening prayer found in the session and have everyone read it aloud together.

Scripture Reading

Luke 24:13–35

Ask a member of the group to read, or you can read it aloud to the group. Once the passage is read, direct the group members to silently reflect for a minute or two on what they have just heard. This also serves as a centering and quieting exercise for participants.

Supporting catechism quotes for Session Ten

"[Christ's] Paschal mystery...is unique: all other historical events happen once, and then they pass away....The Paschal mystery of Christ, by contrast...transcends all times while being made present in them all. The event of the Cross and Resurrection abides and draws everything toward life" (CCC 1085); Romans 6:10; Hebrews 7:27 and 9:12; see John 13:1 and 17:1.

"[Christ] is present when the Church prays and sings, for he has promised 'where two or three are gathered together in my name there am I in the midst of them'" (CCC 1088); Matthew 18:20.

"In the liturgy of the New Covenant every liturgical action, especially the celebration of the Eucharist and the sacraments, is an encounter between Christ and the Church" (CCC 1097).

"Once again it is the Holy Spirit who gives the grace of faith, strengthens it and makes it grow in the community. The liturgical assembly is first of all a communion in faith" (CCC 1102).

Liturgy

ALLOW FIFTEEN MINUTES FOR EACH SECTION.

Take a few minutes for the group to read through the section, then move to the **LOVE in Action** questions. Allow each person a minute or two to contribute, and give each group member the opportunity to speak.

Additional questions for reflection and discussion

- *In what ways does the liturgy "form" or influence those who participate in it? In what ways do you think it has "formed" you? Or has it?*

- *Why do you think Christ commanded us to celebrate the Eucharist in his memory? Why was it so important to him?*

- *Why is the yearning of the ancient Hebrews for a Messiah so important to the overall story of our salvation?*

- *What things, forces, or attitudes might stand in the way of our truly becoming the body of Christ in the Eucharist?*

- *What other ways, besides those named, can the liturgy model for us a just and peaceful society?*

- *Does the union of all believers—our transformation into one body in Christ—ever make you feel uncomfortable? What are the challenges of such unity?*

Closing Rite

FIVE MINUTES

Conclude the lesson by praying the Lord's Prayer:

Our Father, who art in heaven,
hallowed be thy name;
thy kingdom come;
thy will be done on earth as it is in heaven.
Give us this day our daily bread;
and forgive us our trespasses
as we forgive those who trespass against us;
and lead us not into temptation,
but deliver us from evil. Amen.

Ask the participants for spontaneous prayer.

When finished you can offer this brief blessing to the group:

The LORD bless you and keep you!

The LORD let his face shine upon you, and be gracious to you!

The LORD look upon you kindly and give you peace! (Numbers 6: 24–26)

Closing Song: "One Bread, One Body," by John Foley, or a hymn of your choice

Concluding Prayer: Ever-loving God, you give us all we need. You created our hearts for love and sustain them in love through the sacraments of your Church. Help us to grow in faith and holiness through our learning and discussion today. Be with us on our pilgrimage toward greater holiness, and bring us at last to your heavenly kingdom. We ask this through Christ, our Lord. Amen.

SESSION 10

Liturgy as a Form of Community Prayer and Manifestation of God's Love

By Emily Strand, MA

WHO is called to the Church's liturgical celebrations?

WHAT do we mean by "liturgical prayer?"

WHERE does the way we pray together, particularly the Mass, come from?

WHEN do Catholics gather to pray the liturgy, and what do they celebrate?

WHY does it matter whether Catholics celebrate the liturgy or not?

Opening Song: "Lord, Who at Thy First Eucharist," by William H. Turton, or a hymn of your choice

Opening Prayer: God of love, you have revealed to us the heart of truth in the paschal mystery of your Son Jesus. Open our minds to the mystery of faith we celebrate in the liturgy. Help us, through our learning and discussion, to receive the fullness of your grace in the Eucharist. Through our participation in your Church's liturgy, bring us closer to you and to one another. We ask this through Christ your Son, in the unity of the Holy Spirit: one God forever and ever. Amen.

Reading: Luke 24:13–35 (Jesus' appearance on the road to Emmaus)

Spend a moment in quiet reflection.

Liturgical Prayer

"Liturgy" is a word some people find intimidating, perhaps because the word is new to them, or because they do not know exactly what it refers to. It is a word Catholics use to distinguish a certain type of structured, communal prayer from personal, spontaneous, or devotional prayer. While personal prayer is often formed by an individual in a particular moment of need (as in "God help me!"), liturgical prayer has a way of forming us, both as individuals and as a community of believers.

Liturgy often refers specifically to the Mass, or the celebration of the Eucharist. Liturgy actually can refer to any form of structured, communal prayer, such as a penance service or a wedding. Finally, liturgy can refer to the Divine Office, or the *Liturgy of the Hours*, which is an ancient, pre-scribed way of praying with Psalms and other Scripture through the various times of the day. It is traditionally used in religious communities but is open to all Catholics. In this lesson, we will focus on liturgy as it refers to the Mass.

The word "liturgy" is from the Greek word *leitourgia,* which means public works, or the infrastructure supporting the life of a society. Like roads, bridges, plumbing, and electricity, liturgy supports the life of the body of Christ in its relationship with God. All relationships need infrastructure: friends hang out together, couples go on dates, families gather for the evening meal. Without such support structures, relationships suffer. In a sense, liturgy is the Church's weekly "date" with God. It is mutually desirable time spent together by people who love one another deeply.

But why must liturgy be the form our "date" with God takes every week? Does it really matter to God what we do, as long as we spend quality time together? Yes and no. Of course God wants to be with us—with each of us—in any way we offer. Our personal and devotional prayer is a key component to our spiritual lives. But God, through Christ, invites us to become one with him, and with one another in a unique way through the Eucharist. Of course he wants us to pray every day, but he was talking about the Eucharist when he commanded us to "do this in memory of me."

> *Liturgical prayer has a way of forming us, both as individuals and as a community of believers.*

Why We Pray This Way

This commandment by Jesus for us to celebrate the Eucharist in his memory comes from Gospel accounts of the Last Supper and forms the starting point of the Mass. Jesus' disciples obeyed him faithfully, celebrating the Eucharist as he taught them in small groups, which quickly began to grow. Soon the Breaking of the Bread (as the Mass was known) was the heart of a new movement in the Mediterranean world of the first centuries: the Christian movement. This ancient Eucharist was different in many ways from what Catholics experience today. It was held secretly in humble places or homes, and its prayers were often improvised. The structure of the ancient Eucharist was simpler and could differ from community to community, and singing probably played an even bigger role than it does today. But the core of the celebration was the same as now: the breaking open of the Scriptures followed by the Breaking of the Bread.

The Jewish prayer traditions of Jesus and his followers, as well as the Greco-Roman culture in which they lived, are the cultural foundations of the Mass. But as the Mass moved beyond the cultures of its birth, it changed and developed. The Church was no longer a persecuted minority, but the state religion. The separation of the Eastern Church from the Church of Rome gave Western European cultures considerable influence over its development. As the Mass continued to move West, it collected rituals, prayers, and other additions from the many cultures with which it came into contact.

The Mass has been through 2,000 years of historical development—years that came with a lot of liturgical baggage! The Second Vatican Council in the 1960s helped to reform the Mass, which had become cluttered with ritual, and to restore the participative quality it had possessed in the ancient Church. The council also sought to make Mass more "catholic" (a word that means "universal") by making room for the languages, cultural symbols, and traditions of the many peoples of the world who celebrate it. To achieve this, the council mandated major reforms to the liturgy. The result was a "new" Mass that was in graceful continuity with the way in which the Eucharist was celebrated by the early Christians so long ago. And the essence of the Mass was again made clear: our participation in the paschal mystery of Christ.

LOVE in Action

- *What do you think of when you hear the word "liturgy?" Is it a familiar or new word to you? Does thinking of liturgy as infrastructure enhance its meaning for you? How?*

- *How does liturgical prayer differ from personal or devotional prayer for you?*

- *What do you feel when you hear that the core of the Mass today is much the same as when it was celebrated by Christians in the first centuries?*

- *In what ways do you think moving from persecuted minority to state religion changed the Church and its liturgy?*

- *Why is it important for the Mass to be "catholic" (meaning "universal")?*

The Lord's Day: What We Celebrate

The four Gospel accounts agree that the resurrection of Christ occurred on the first day of the week. To the Jews this was Sunday, the day after the Sabbath, and Sunday came to have a special significance to Christians. They saw it as a day outside of time itself. Sunday was a day for miracles—a day penetrated with the saving power of God. These Jewish-Christians viewed Sunday in the light of Psalm 118: as a day made by the Lord himself, a day for rejoicing. Truly this was the Lord's Day. It is no wonder that they chose to celebrate the Eucharist on this glorious, miraculous day.

It was a glorious, miraculous mystery they celebrated on the Lord's Day so long ago, and that same mystery is at the center of our modern eucharistic liturgy. In fact, the Second Vatican Council's main document on liturgy, *Sacrosanctum Concilium*, says the Church has never not come together to celebrate the mystery of our faith: the paschal mystery. But what do we mean by "paschal mystery?" What is this mystery that forms the heart of the praying Church?

Catholics well educated in the faith may feel able to answer this question right away. "The paschal mystery," they might say, "refers to the life, death, and resurrection of Christ." They may also say "paschal mystery" refers to the Easter mysteries, or captures the essential aspects of our redemption in Christ. In all these answers, they are correct. But "paschal mystery" is a phrase so full of significance that we could spend the rest of this lesson—indeed our whole lives—unpacking it. The above answers, although correct, are too narrow. They only refer to the events surrounding Jesus' life and do not reveal, as the phrase intends, Christ's place in the whole history of our salvation—from creation to the anticipated Second Coming—including the present. To get a sense for this "big picture" of our salvation in

> *"The paschal mystery refers to the life, death, and resurrection of Christ."*

Christ, which "paschal mystery" describes, let's take the phrase one word at a time.

The word "paschal" refers to the Hebrew Passover, the annual feast which commemorated the Jews' liberation by God, through his servant Moses, from slavery in Egypt, as told in the book of Exodus. In this story, God acts in human history to save his people in response to their cries for freedom. God takes sides against the Egyptians, sending plagues and signs against them, and empowers a Hebrew—Moses, a reluctant but ultimately successful leader—to free his people from their bondage to Pharaoh. At Moses' command, the Hebrews mark themselves with the blood of a lamb to escape the plague of death and are led miraculously through the sea on dry land to escape Pharaoh's army.

It is a fantastic, heroic tale—and yet its results are incomplete. The freed Hebrews wander in the desert for forty years searching for their Promised Land, only to find that it is occupied! They grumble against God and fail in their test of faith. But the Passover, the annual remembrance of God freeing them from slavery in Egypt, taught them to hope: in perfect freedom, prosperity, and in a perfect, new Moses, who would someday lead them out of every type of bondage—even death. The Passover of the Lord was a feast of hopeful expectation for the Jews. It taught them to yearn for the Messiah.

It was to a Jewish people shaped by this Passover hope that Jesus of Nazareth preached, taught, healed, and ministered. But let's not get ahead of ourselves—first we have to talk about the word "mystery" in "paschal mystery."

Modern people, shaped by murder-mystery books, films, and TV, tend to think of a "mystery" as something we humans should solve. On TV, a mystery is a conundrum that is satisfyingly deciphered in about an hour. This is not how the word functions in the phrase "paschal mystery." "Mystery" in our all-important phrase refers to the vast, inscrutable life of God, into which we are invited through Christ, in the power of the Holy Spirit. That's right: this life of God to which the word "mystery" refers is Trinitarian life: a life of Father, Son, and Holy Spirit. Let's take a brief look at the "mystery" of each.

The mystery of God the Father, the first person of the Holy Trinity, refers to God's plan for our salvation, which is known and understood by God alone. This great story of our salvation (also known as salvation history) began at the beginning; God created us and our world in order to save us. And it will end at the ending: the Second Coming foretold in the Book of Revelation. (It helps to remember that the Bible, which begins with Genesis and ends with the Book of Revelation, tells this story of our salvation.)

Although God's plan for our salvation is full of mystery, it has been revealed to us in Christ, the second person of the Trinity. The mystery of Christ is the heart of the paschal mystery. Through Christ's life, death, and resurrection we are redeemed to God and freed from the bondage of our human mortality forever. Christ is the new Adam, who, "though he was in the form of God" (Philippians 2:6), chose humility over godliness. And bringing the word "paschal" together with the word "mystery," Christ is the long-awaited new Moses, who

obeys God without reluctance, leading his people not to earthly freedom, but to liberation from sin and death. No longer can these things separate us from God, nor from one another.

And in a mysterious new way, Christ is the Passover Lamb of God, who, in his innocence and willingness to die for all, shows us love in its most radical form. In the loving self-sacrifice of Christ, we are saved from death itself. Above all else, this saving love is what Christians gather to celebrate in the Eucharist on Sundays.

LOVE in Action

- *What is Sunday like for you and your family? Is it a special day? How? Or is it just like any other?*

- *Is the phrase "paschal mystery" new to you or familiar? If familiar, what were your impressions of its meaning?*

- *Why do we say Christ is the "new Adam?" The "new Moses?" The "Lamb of God?"*

Called to the Table

There is one more aspect of the word "mystery" in "paschal mystery" to consider: the mystery of the Church. If you've been closely following this Trinitarian explanation of the word "mystery," you may wonder why I didn't say "the mystery of the Holy Spirit," the third member of the Trinity. It is because the mystery of the Church is the mystery of the Holy Spirit in the phrase "paschal mystery." Through the Holy Spirit, we become a Church called to celebrate and perpetuate this mystery of our faith.

This third aspect of the word "mystery" is the bridge over which the story of our salvation comes into our hearts and teaches us how to live. Catholics often refer to the people who gather for Sunday liturgy as the "assembly." The Greek root of this word means those who are called, and this defines the liturgical assembly on the Lord's Day: those who are called by God (that would be everyone!), and those who have answered the call (sadly, not as many). The call to what? To be part of the great story of salvation, the heart of which we celebrate in the Eucharist: the paschal mystery.

We first become part of this story of radical love—of dying to selfish desires and rising to new life in Christ —by answering the call, by coming to Mass. In this act, we give up our desire to sleep in or to catch up on work on Sundays, and instead we say "yes" to the community's celebration. Our involvement in the story deepens by our full, conscious, and active participation at Mass through our heartfelt praying and singing. Even our gestures, postures, listening, and processing—in union with the praying assembly—tell of our new life of love and service in Christ.

But the most important way we take part in the paschal mystery of Christ each Sunday is by partaking of his Body and Blood in the Eucharist. Catholics believe that the bread and wine at Communion are transformed in their essence (if not in their properties) into the Body and Blood of Christ—a reality called transubstantiation. Through this meal, we who are called to the table are also transformed from our imperfect selves to the people God made us to be. Our lives may be broken, our sin may be persistent, but in the Eucharist we catch a glimpse of how we will be when we sit at the heavenly banquet with all the saints. As Saint Augustine taught, in the Eucharist, we receive who we are meant to be in God's eyes, and we become what we receive. We become the body of Christ.

LOVE in Action

- *How is the Church related to the Holy Spirit in your understanding? Do we ever forget this? Why?*

- *What is your level of participation in Mass? Do you ever feel you could participate more fully? How?*

- *Does the full meaning of receiving the Eucharist —that is, our becoming the Body and Blood of Christ—ever seem intimidating to you? Why or why not?*

Manifesting God's Love in the World

Have you ever wondered where the Mass gets its name? The answer tells of an important connection between liturgy and life. In the original Latin, the very last line of the Mass was *"Ite, missa est"* which basically meant "you are dismissed." However, the word *missa* had a richer meaning back then than "dismissal" does today. It had connotations of "being sent," as on an important mission (a similarly derived word). The mission, of course, is the work of the body of Christ, to which each person who dines at the eucharistic table is called. We Catholics have named our worship, not for what we do within it, but for the mission of paschal mystery living on which it sends us when it is complete.

The answer to the question "why does it matter whether Catholics celebrate liturgy or not?" is interwoven with the power of the Mass to send us forth on mission. Our worship, rightly observed, has the power to direct our lives, even our society, toward justice and peace. In fact, Pope John Paul II said the Eucharist we celebrate in Mass does not merely bring us, as individuals, into the life of the Church, but is a "project of solidarity" for the entire human family (*Mane nobiscum Domine* 27).

The liturgy accomplishes this in many ways. The Scripture readings and homily help us hear the word of God and live his desire "that they may all be one" (John 17:21). In the General Intercessions, we stand before God in prayer, both for our own needs and those of the world. The processions of the Mass reveal us to be a pilgrim people, imperfect and imperiled, but always one, and ever growing in holiness on our journey home to God. In the sign of peace, we extend forgiveness and friendship to all, even strangers. More than anything, our sharing in the Eucharist transforms us and all believers into one body in Christ, and gives us a glimpse of our heavenly home where we will be one in God. No longer are we a group of "I's"; now we are a "we," with Christ as our head. This means we must care for one another to preserve our very self. Seen in this light, the answer to "why go to Mass" is obvious: Who would we be without it? Although all prayer is valuable, no other form of prayer (personal prayer, devotions, etc.) has the power of the Eucharist to form us into the body of Christ.

This body of Christ—this Church—is the means by which God's love is manifested in the world. By celebrating the paschal mystery of Christ's death and resurrection, Christians are given the grace to show the world what love truly is. And to reveal this love is to reveal God, for "God is love, and whoever remains in love remains in God and God in him" (1 John 4:16).

LOVE in Action

- *Do you think of Mass as sending you on a "mission?" What kind of mission?*

- *Is it important to you that Catholics celebrate Mass regularly? Why or why not?*

- *In what ways do you share the love of God with the world?*

Closing Song: "One Bread, One Body," by John Foley, or a hymn of your choice

Concluding Prayer: Ever-loving God, you give us all we need. You created our hearts for love and sustain them in love through the sacraments of your Church. Help us to grow in faith and holiness through our learning and discussion today. Be with us on our pilgrimage toward greater holiness, and bring us at last to your heavenly kingdom. We ask this through Christ, our Lord. Amen.

SUGGESTED RESOURCES:

The Liturgy Documents Volume One: Fourth Edition (Liturgy Training Publications, 2007).

Johnson, Lawrence J. *The Mystery of Faith: Revised Edition*

Moroney, Msgr. James P. *The Mass Explained: Revised and Expanded Edition* (Catholic Book Publishing, 2008).

Strand, Emily. *Mass 101: Liturgy and Life.*

CINEMA CONNECTION

A River Runs Through It (1992), starring Craig Sheffer, Brad Pitt, Tom Skerritt. A story of the lives of two young men in rural Montana.

Il Postino (1994), in Italian with English subtitles, starring Philippe Noiret, Massimo Troisi, Maria Grazia. An Italian postman befriends a famous poet by delivering mail to his home. The friendship enlivens both and enables the postman to fall in love as he discovers poetry.

ABOUT THE AUTHOR

Emily Strand, MA, was campus minister and director of liturgy at the University of Dayton for seven years, where she also taught courses on Catholicism and Catholic liturgy. Now a full-time mom, Emily serves on the Worship Commission for the Archdiocese of Cincinnati, speaks at parishes on liturgy and the paschal mystery, and serves her parish in Columbus, Ohio, as a lector and choir member.

Notes

Notes

Notes

Notes

Notes

Notes

Notes

Notes

Notes

Notes

Notes

CPSIA information can be obtained at www.ICGtesting.com
Printed in the USA
LVOW09s2350111013

356621LV00002B/5/P

9 780764 823985